From Hell's Heart

From Hell's Heart

A Memoir of Holocaust Survivors and Their Son

SAMUEL S. BRUNER

Copyright © 2015 Samuel S. Bruner
All rights reserved.

ISBN: 1511888245
ISBN 13: 9781511888240
Library of Congress Control Number: 2015913410
CreateSpace Independent Publishing Platform
North Charleston, South Carolina

This book is dedicated first to my mother, a woman who is strong, gentle, wise, kind, shrewd, and loving to all the children she has had a chance to be close to. Her support has always given me strength, and she taught me to be fearless in face of what life had to throw at me.

To my wife, Deborah, an example to women everywhere, who went to a local state college for a degree in nursing in part because of her caring nature and also because it was a good field for a woman if she had to support herself. Her constant curiosity and thirst for knowledge led her to become an internationally recognized speaker, writer, and cancer researcher. She worked on her doctorate while working, raising one child, and preparing for the birth of another. Her example was an inspiration to me. She was the strongest supporter of my decision to get my graduate degree and start a second career a bit later than most people.

To my Aunt Halina, whom I have loved and admired since childhood. She entered the Plaszow concentration camp at age thirteen. Most children of that age died or were murdered. With a powerful will to live and by the kindness of Oskar Schindler, she survived. While running a household and raising three children, she became an independent, successful businesswoman. She fills her days with college lectures, exercise, field trips, and speaking about the Shoah to private and government agencies in the Baltimore/Washington area. Her appreciation of each new day as a gift is an example to us all.

To my brother, Joe, my friend since childhood, mentor, and longtime business partner, who I know would have been proud of me for writing this book. I will always miss him.

To my sons, cousins, and friends, who all said, "You should write a book."

Acknowledgments

Thank you to Bruce Marcoon, my high-school English and literature teacher. He encouraged me throughout this project. He read, corrected, and critiqued it, and he pushed me to finish this manuscript and pushed me again to finally publish it. It is no wonder he has thousands of Facebook friends, almost all of whom are former students.

Thank you again to Aunt Halina, who gave me hours of her time filling in historical gaps and resurrecting painful memories so that I could finish this story.

To my Uncle Gerry for his support and help in understanding the struggle involved in building the young State of Israel, based on his personal experiences and relationships with other heroes such as David Ben-Gurion, Moshe Dayan, Ariel Sharon, and Chaim Bar-Lev.

Foreword

Years ago, when I first met Sam Bruner as one of my students, I sensed something special about him. Reuniting decades later, I knew that my initial perception was right.

From Hell's Heart has literally been raked from the ashes of the Holocaust. Sam has masterfully recounted the relevant history and the causes and effects as they affected his parents, other family members, and ultimately himself. The reader emerges with an understanding rarely experienced in writings of this genre. Questions that might occur in the reader's mind are answered before they arise.

Stylistically, the book is amazing. The imagery allows it to unfold almost as a verbal motion picture. (It would certainly make a great film.) The connotative aspect created with figurative language widens the view of the reader. The editorial-type commentary clearly shows what the writer is thinking. Especially impressive is the manner in which Sam actually assumes the personae of various family members and speaks for them as they move through the pertinent stages of their lives. The reader totally understands their thoughts and actions as they experience the fateful events as they happen and then the results of those events years later.

Sam's intellectual grasp of the times and the resultant impact on those lives shows incredible insight into and understanding of the workings of the human mind. His historical knowledge provides a framework that gives deeper understanding to the reader. This is a story that had to be told. It is an important piece of writing on multiple levels and from many perspectives. The insight gained is also important to understanding the world of today.

It is, of course, a personal saga. Sam's life with his mother, father, and other family members shows the cumulative effects as they filter down, ultimately resulting in the Sam Bruner of today—an admirable man who has dedicated his life to trying to make life better for the people he meets, particularly the less fortunate.

Those ashes still smolder, giving off a guiding light. If Sam were still my student, he would receive an A plus. Sam Bruner has not just written a book; this is actually a terrific piece of literature.

Bruce L. Marcoon

Contents

One

MEIN KAMPF

Heaven have mercy on us all—
Presbyterians and Pagans alike
—for we are all somehow dreadfully cracked about the head,
—and sadly need mending.

—HERMAN MELVILLE, *MOBY-DICK*

H is index finger was bent over, with the middle knuckle sticking up. The knuckle and part of the finger were in his mouth, his teeth clenched down over the flesh. I couldn't hear him breathing out, but I could see his chest expand and hear him rapidly sucking air in. He looked at me with the wildest eyes I had ever seen. It wasn't him. That was not the father I knew. Not that his stare wasn't piercing; it was only that I had never seen this look before. I was afraid he would hit me next. I screamed and cried, but I was too scared to tell him again to stop.

I was five years old, and it was 1960. My brothers and sister had gone off to school. My father should have been at work. My mother should have gotten me ready for the kindergarten bus. But I wasn't going to school on this day. I felt guilty for not getting a knife and using it on him.

Not because I hated him or wanted to harm him; I didn't. I just wanted him to stop hitting my mother.

He turned from me and hit my mother in the face again. The finger went back in his mouth, and the heavy breathing happened again. My mother screamed back at him, but I could not understand Polish. My parents spoke to me in English and to each other in Polish. Mom stood up and yelled at Dad some more. Dad picked up a chair and came at her. She turned away, and he smashed it across her back. Things died down quickly after that. Perhaps he realized he had crossed a line.

Mom moved to the living-room sofa. I curled up next to her. The fight had unfolded so quickly. I had not seen it before. I was upset and scared, but at the same time, I was a detached observer. Was this normal? Was this how all families were?

Eventually Dad came out of the bedroom dressed for work. He said some words to her in a kind tone. She did not answer. He smiled and asked me if I was mad at him. I said nothing. I just huddled closer to my mother and glared at him. I had never seen my mother with a black eye before. He turned toward the front door, took a step, and stopped. He turned around and pulled a pack of Life Savers out of his pocket. Dad had a sweet tooth. He waved it at me. I jumped off the couch, snatched it from his hand, and cuddled up against my mother. My father smiled a sly smile that showed off his gold-capped tooth. He turned and went out the door. I immediately felt guilty. I should never have taken it. I had betrayed my mother for a pack of Life Savers. It wasn't even chocolate.

Mom spent most of the day in bed, sobbing. I lay next to her, and she hugged me the whole time. I kept trying to tell her it would be all right. After a few hours, I got up to watch TV. I threw the Life Savers away. I could not understand why I had taken them. Mom got them out of the trash and told me it was OK to eat them.

My siblings came home from school and saw the wreckage in the bedroom. I was afraid to tell them what had happened. But they knew. They had seen this before. Dad was actually getting better. I did not know it, but the fights were becoming less frequent. My siblings had seen worse.

They were used to seeing the large wedding picture that hung above my parents' bed lying on the floor with the glass smashed. I don't know how many times that glass was smashed. I can tell you that the picture must have been made of some tough material, because no matter how many times the glass was broken, the picture always still looked like new.

People walk around that way. They look like new, and we never know how many times the glass has broken. I guess they learn to close one eye. Otherwise, they would never make it.

All four of the Bruner children witnessed these beatings. They affected us all differently. No. It wasn't the Shoah.[1] In my house, you did not have problems, because you didn't go through the war. Everything else was small potatoes. The dysfunctional families they came from affected all the children of Shoah survivors. Like the survivors themselves, the manifestations of their symptoms varied based upon their psychological predisposition. Some cried and were very emotional, some suffered from depression, some were mentally abusive, and some became cold and hard, but no one remained unscarred.

Why should I tell this story and besmirch the reputation of a dead man who accomplished many good things in his life? A man who came to America with no language skills, minimal education, no money. A man who never wanted a penny from the government and only accepted a small amount of charity at the beginning so his children would have some food, clothes, and a roof for a few months.

How many times over the course of history, in how many families, has there been, is now, and will be domestic violence? The number is unfathomable. More importantly, how many did not go through something as unimaginably terrifying and scarring as the Shoah? Did they have a better excuse? There is no excuse, but there is understanding and forgiveness. If my mother forgave my father, how could I not?

What is most important about Dad's character was that he stopped. Not all at once. But he gained control of himself. I have no doubt that he was able to remove himself from the situation and realize that a family

---

1 See Appendix.

could not go on this way and survive. In Proverbs 11:29, it says that one who brings trouble to his home shall inherit the wind, and the fool will be the servant to the wise. I believe my father had enough sense that he did not want to inherit the wind.

In domestic violence, there is something called the circle of control. If the circle continues unchecked, the inevitable result is violence. In my work as a family attorney, from my experiences dealing with domestic violence, I can say that he did not fit the profile. He did not come home drunk; he did not gamble away the family's money; he did not want to know where we were every minute of the day; he did not have jealous fits when others complimented my mother on her natural beauty; he did not explode into violent rages over the wrong word.

I would be letting him off too easily if I said the violence was simply situational. Yet, it could be predictable. He learned to control himself, and we learned what would usually set him off. He was disappointed and frustrated. He was frustrated that his business was not taking off faster. He was disappointed that my mother no longer looked up to him the way she had when they were first married. As to his disappointment in his marriage, he advised us that when you fall in love, you are wearing rose-colored glasses. After you are married, the glasses come off, and, of course, you have to learn to close one eye. He had so many sayings about how to get through life, not just the one about closing one eye. He often let us make our own mistakes. He tried to guide our development, generally, but not control it. He said a father should not try too hard. There is no payoff. He said that a father can support ten sons, but ten sons could not support one father. He was no scholar; he didn't know it came from the Talmud. He was raised around a lot of Yiddish sayings without knowing their actual source. It was the words that mattered to him.

Sometimes good things can come out of a bad situation. I felt very close to my mother and very protective. She wanted to protect me, too, and often stood between my father and me. There was only so much she could do, but it became a sort of mutual protection, and I don't think we would have shared the degree of closeness we had if my father had not been abusive.

Some people just repeat their parents' mistakes. As I got older, I saw things that I did not want to repeat. I know it made me a better husband and father. Now, as I practice law and incorporate domestic violence into my practice, I am sure I am a better counselor because of it. Recently I helped a woman get a protection order against her spouse. He was abusing her in front of her son. She was worried about her son. He was acting up in school (just as I did). He wanted to move in with his father because he thought his father would then leave his mother alone.

The father never had the sense to know that when he beat the mother in front of her son, he might as well as have been beating his son, whom he had never physically hurt. I explained to her that her son was trying to protect her, just as she was trying to protect him; that there was some special good that would come out of this, and that she and her son could become very close, as I had with my mother. Her eyes welled with tears. She held my hand and thanked me. I am pretty sure that a lot of attorneys would not come up with those words. What had happened to me has given me a talent for understanding these issues. I continue to take these cases, and I find it meaningful. I think it is my penance for taking the Life Savers.

Sunday was the only day the store was closed. Sometimes the family did things together. It was more like my mother telling my father to take the kids somewhere so she could get the housework done. My mother worked in the store with my father during the week and on Saturday, so she needed Sunday to get the housework done and make the chicken soup that would nourish us all week long. One of the things we liked to do was go to the movies. That was a time when you went into the city to see a big-screen theater. My brother Joe scanned the paper for potential movies. One of the movies was called *Mein Kampf*.[2] It was 1961, and this was the first movie documentary that included a compilation of Nazi footage showing their murderous actions. Much of the movie showed

---

2 See Appendix.

footage of concentration-camp victims, dead and alive, including the bulldozing of bodies and mass graves. It came down to two movies and a vote. Although much of my father's running of the family was "his way or the highway," he could also decide to be very democratic. My father and Joe wanted to see *Mein Kampf*. Harry, Gena, and I wanted to see the other movie.

Joe took me aside into my parents' bedroom. He opened a drawer, reached under the clothes and into the back, and took out a yellow envelope. He pulled out the black-and-white glossy pictures. These were pictures given to my father by the American army after Nuremberg. They were pictures of Nazi leaders who had been hung, lying on stone slabs. The ropes were cut, so the nooses were still around their necks, except for Goering, who had committed suicide in his cell. Each body had a white banner across the chest with the name. All the big names were there. Joe told me that if we went to see *Mein Kampf*, we could see lots of dead people. At seven years old, that clinched it for me. Not only did the children's movie sound cheesy compared to this, but Joe was my older brother, and I looked up to him. If he said this was going to be cool, then I believed him. I cast the deciding vote.

This was a three-hour movie, and as the hours wound by, I was becoming inured to the footage of Hitler screaming during his speeches, bonfires, war scenes, and even the gruesome camp pictures. My father said he was in camps, but I always thought that was where he swam and played soccer in the summertime. He didn't look like any of these people, so it must not have been these camps. I was getting bored; I wanted to know when it would be over. I wanted a soda. I didn't understand everything. I sat next to my father and kept asking him questions. He kept shushing me over and over and never responded.

Finally, his curled index finger went into his mouth and he sucked in the air. After the experience of watching him hit my mother, I thought he was about to slap me, so I shut up real quick. He wasn't going to slap me at all. It was the footage of the camps. Only years later did I learn that shoving his finger in his mouth and sucking in was his way of not screaming out loud at the sight of mass shootings, the sadistic killings, and being one of the people who had to dig up the rotted corpses of Russian prisoners who were executed at Plaszow. He was not aware of the times I had seen him do it, and he wasn't aware that he had done it since the war. It was then that I realized that although there are no excuses for domestic violence, the war did things to him that he could never learn to control.

Two

Roots

"Is this how you repay my goodness—
with badness?" cried the boy.
"Of course," said the crocodile out of the corner of his mouth.
"That is the way of the world."

—ALEX HALEY, *Roots*

"I don't know why they show this on TV. Why do they have to dredge up such an ugly past? People get the wrong idea about America from this," my father complained.

"Why is it OK to watch one show after another about World War II, when the Germans would like to forget? Why shouldn't black people want everyone to know what was done to them when the Jews certainly do?" Joe and I both asked.

"It was different," my father said every week while *Roots* was shown on TV. "We wished we could be slaves. They had children. We would have sold our future generations into slavery to avoid extermination. Slaves had value, like farm animals. How badly could they have been treated?"

It turns out they were treated pretty badly. Most importantly, they did not know who they were. They lost their culture, religion, language, history…in essence, what it is that makes a people a people, proud of their heritage. Yes, they were Americans, but for the most part, they did not share in the dream. You cannot compare the Shoah to anything in history, but that does not mean that other people did not suffer or that their suffering did not mean as much to them. For Africans brought to America, it was their heritage that was exterminated. The Jews of Europe did one of two things. Some turned inward to their religion, arguing the fine points of the Talmud and creating more rules to live by. They brought order to chaos. It reminds me of children who grow up in homes that are chaotic. They grow up trying to control their environment, trying to bring order to chaos. Rules helped the community to survive. They created so many rules to live by that there was little time in the day for contemplation of the oppression around them.

Though I know of no statistics regarding assimilation, it seems that, based on the long history of the Jews and the population growth of other European populations, we should be, as God told Abraham, as numerous as the stars in the heavens regardless of the numbers that were killed over time. The answer for most was conversion or assimilation, to the point where Jews became so secularized over several generations that stepping over to Christianity or Islam became a small change.

The point is that both of these answers allowed for either the survival of the culture or integration for those who chose (or were forced) to be a part of the wider world. American blacks did not have this choice. Their culture was lost, and assimilation was not possible because they could not change the color of their skin.

The concept behind Zionism is that Jews would never be accepted in Europe, so they needed to find a land of their own. Blacks had the "Back to Africa" movement, but Africa is a continent. They had little to tie them to a homeland, no common language and history to tie them to one another, no culture separate from their American culture. Their culture was American. It was African American. They knew only this land, but they were never either prepared or allowed to participate in its fullness.

So what is it about the Jews that made their suffering so much more terrible than other people's that they would write innumerable books; lay claim to Palestine for their own; and create museums in Israel, Washington, DC, and Berlin, along with many other places? Why publish a book on the subject when so much has been written that many Jews and non-Jews have grown tired of reading about it, using the argument that there are so many other people in this world who also suffered? Did the Armenians or Cambodians suffer any less?

I have my own answer. I do not for one moment denigrate the sufferings of others. If just one family loses a beloved member, there is suffering. Does it really matter to a family whether a terrorist kills an Israeli child or a Palestinian child dies from collateral damage resulting from an attack on a legitimate military target? The fact remains that a child is dead, and the family will suffer for a long time.

The history of the Jews is unique and worthy of study, not because their lives were more valuable than others but because of the unique circumstances. They were allowed to immigrate to countries—they were even invited because of the skills they brought with them that resulted in prosperity wherever they lived. They believed in the sanctity of contracts, the rule of law, self-governing communities, obedience and loyalty to the laws, and sovereignty of the nations they inhabited. Many of them integrated, spoke the local language, did business with their non-Jewish neighbors and fought in their armies. Yet at some point, in most of the nations in Europe, they were eventually the victims and scapegoats, accused of conspiracy to bring down the nation, murdering non-Jewish children for their religious rituals, and they were always reminded at Easter of their culpability in deicide.

Had it not been for the Roman emperor Constantine, there would be no Jews or Christians in Europe. It was Constantine who chose Christianity as the religion of the empire. There were others. Mithraism, an outgrowth of the Persian religion of Zoroastrianism, was very popular. There was good and evil, the promise of a messiah, and many other parallels to Christianity. Had Constantine chosen this religion, there would have been no conversion allowed to Christianity or Judaism. Instead, by choosing Christianity, the church fathers were left with a dilemma. They could not ignore the fact that Jesus was a Jew and their heritage stemmed from Judaism. As Christians gained power, members of other sects were pressured and finally forced to convert. What to do about the Jews? Some church leaders believed they should be treated like the others: convert, leave, or be killed. Others, most notably Saint Augustine, believed the Jews had a special place. They should survive but not thrive. They should be allowed to live, but only in a state of wretchedness as an example to others of the consequences of rejecting the divinity of Christ. This created a problem, as the Jews refused to be wretched and instead thrived and prospered in Christian lands. How could God reward these Christ-killers? What kind of example would this be to Christians who also questioned church doctrine? For the church, things were not working out according to plan. The Jews were reined in at different times, whether by popular uprising instigated by the church or the nobility, or by a king who was particularly religious (such as Louis IX of France, who became Saint Louis), or fanatical leaders of the church in different countries such as the Dominicans of Spain, led by Torquemada.

Jews were often a popular scapegoat for the church or the nobles when things went badly. Jews were blamed for the Black Death and hunted down and murdered. Pope Clement VI eventually put a stop to it when his investigation showed that Jews were dying in the same proportions as Christians. Jews were restricted to certain professions, including moneylending. Nobles who borrowed money to make war had to raise taxes on the peasants. When the peasants revolted, the nobles blamed the Jews. The Jews were killed or exiled, leaving the nobles debt-free.

The stereotypes became a pervasive part of European culture. Shakespeare wrote *The Merchant of Venice,* using a moneylending, greedy Jew named Shylock as the antagonist, even though Jews had not lived in

England for hundreds of years and would not return until well after his death. It is unlikely that he ever knew a Jew in his lifetime.

Why study or read about the Shoah? It was the final culmination of all this history. From the perspective of my parents, persecution, pogroms, discrimination, degradation, and even forced conversion was the price we paid for remaining Jews in a Christian world. This is what made the idea of extermination an unbelievable threat by the Nazis. If, after all these centuries, extermination had never been the goal in the darkest of times, how could it happen now in the twentieth century? Discrimination in America was not even worth discussing. We were still free to create our own universities, hospitals, and means of employment. Extermination was the unique invention of the Nazis. Other forms of subhumans would be depopulated, and a remnant would be allowed to survive. Only the Jews would be entirely liquidated down to the last man, woman, and child. Slavery and conversion were not the answer. The destruction of the religion and culture was not the answer. The Jews were too clever. They would only rise again. Right to the end of the war, when trains were needed to bring men and supplies to the front or evacuate the wounded, they were diverted to transport the Jews to their deaths. It did not matter where they lived in this world. In time, the Nazis would attempt to hunt them all down and exterminate every last one of them.

Three

THE WORLD AS IT WAS:
MATES BRUNER

As long as the heart within
A Jewish soul still yearns
And beyond, toward the east
An eye scouts Zion
Our hope is not yet missing,
The hope of two thousand years,
To be a free nation in our land,
The land of Zion and Jerusalem.

—TRANSLATION OF "HATIKVAH (THE HOPE)"

I did some dumb things as a kid in Krakow, just as all kids do. Yes, I yelled and smacked my kids for doing some dumb, life- or limb-threatening things. Sometimes I even used a belt to make sure they remembered. I didn't know that I shouldn't slap a child across the face or hit them with a belt. It was just the way I was raised, so I thought that was what I should do. My mother did those things, but I always thought that was a father's job. My father was a kind, religious man who cowered at my domineering mother. As she ladled out the chicken soup (the great

Jewish symbol of love), she also dished out the poison. My father was weak. He was too kind. He was too gentle. He could never make enough money to support the seven of us and the four children from his first wife. There were no kind words for his parents. The daily rant became like white noise. The most important thing was to eat that soup. Soup, potatoes, and dark bread; it was the stuff of life. It was the sustenance that could get you through the winter, sickness, and even the Nazis. It was my mother's domination that was the poison. That is why I always felt a man should control his home, his wife, his children, maybe even his destiny. I only regret that I did not learn to master my temper.

The two stupidest things I did as a child were not really stupid at all. I was just ignorant. I was only told that I was stupid, so that is what I told my kids. "How stupid could you be?" It was rhetorical sarcasm. It was the poison soup I would pass on to my children.

As a young boy, I was curious about the donkey in my neighbor's yard. How much fun it would be to get a big stick and whack it on the rump? The donkey was not amused, and it was at that time that I learned how far back you could fly if a donkey kicked you in the chin. It wasn't just the pain. It left a scar on my chin for the rest of my life.

We didn't have toys to play with. Not like kids today. We made up our own games. My friends and I found a lime pit. We threw the lime at one another, laughing every time we burned someone. You could say it was fun, until a big lump hit me in the eyes, and I felt a burning pain that made the donkey's kick feel like a simple slap from my mother. After the bandages came off my eyes, I found out that I was green and red color-blind. I have been told that it is a congenital condition, but I swear it was from the lime.

I could not stand to see my kids playing for days on end. One day was OK, but not a week and certainly not a whole summer. It was unproductive, and they learned nothing from it. They should work and learn the value of a dollar. Heck, for a dollar, you could buy half of Krakow before the war. At the very least, they should be reading books and not watching that TV for hours on end. TV was good for news, documentaries (the more about the war, the better), and some entertaining though educational shows like *The Walt Disney Hour*. Though Dinah Shore was not educational, you had to watch shows that featured successful Jews. Dinah Shore didn't even look Jewish, any more than Sammy Davis Junior did. Of course, you had to watch every Jewish comedian like Jack Benny and the other borscht-belt fellows. You couldn't ignore them. Bob Hope was the only exception. He was funny enough that he could have been Jewish.

My mother cared for her children deeply. It is just that life was so harsh; you wouldn't survive if you didn't become harsh. Diphtheria was a plague among children after the Polish-Bolshevik war. I had diphtheria as a boy. My mother took me to the hospital. A bottle of medicine was on the table next to my bed in a large ward. My mother left the family and brought a mattress, put it on the floor next to my bed, and stayed at the hospital. Almost as important, she brought chocolates to cheer me up. It was the sweetest luxury I could remember, filling me with a sense of warmth and well-being, and so expensive you only gave it to a very sick child. Schnapps and slivovitz were pale substitutes for the warmth of chocolate.

Mom had to stay by my bed to be sure I got my medicine. Poland (like the rest of Europe) was a class society. My name was Brunengraber, Mates (pronounced mah-tes) Brunengraber. The last name is the Austrian spelling of the German word meaning "well digger." As you can tell, this was not the most illustrious of names. It certainly was no Rothschild, but it was mine. I was also a Jew, a Jew from a family that sprang from well diggers. That was two strikes against me that surely would not guarantee any tender loving care from the Polish hospital staff. Only my mother could ensure that I would get my medicine on time. Only my mother would hound the nurses and doctors to check on me. No one would mourn a poor dead Jewish child in Poland. Only my mother could protect me from that society. That is how I became a young socialist. Lenin was a hero to idealistic youth from all backgrounds. He was a revolutionary, and his name rang louder than that of Che Guevara in Latin America. You could not actively promote socialism. Marshal Pilsudski, the revered leader of our nation, would see to that. Being a communist would definitely get you into a lot of trouble. Socialism was the only way to level the playing field so that a poor Jewish kid could get the same kind of care as a rich Polish kid. I was sure of it at the time. Zionism was a great way to discover socialism or communism without getting into trouble because, on the surface, all you were advocating was a Jewish homeland, and what Pole in his right mind wouldn't want the Jews to leave Poland?

I knew I was a Jew. Not because my home was kosher. Not because I put on tefillin and prayed with my father every day. Not because we walked to shul on Friday night and Saturday, meeting up with other Orthodox along the way. Not because of the ritual meals and holidays. Not because my mother saved money to buy the raisins and sugar to make her own sweet wine for Passover. When these things in a Jewish community surround you, you can forget that you are different. I knew I was a Jew because I went to public school in prewar Poland, and the church ran the schools. Every morning the Jewish children sat in the back rows and respectfully and silently observed the morning mass. I knew it by heart. I did not have to know that I was Jewish. I only had to know that I was not Catholic, and not being Catholic meant not being Polish any more than Dreyfus[3] was really French. It was just pretend. When trouble came, when you had a dispute with a gentile, then you were a Jew. You were not a Pole, not a Frenchman, not a German, not any nationality in Europe. When the French screamed "Kill the Jews" while Dreyfus was court-martialed, it was the turning point for Theodore Herzl,[4] and it was the spark and legend for all young Zionists. At Passover, all Jews were to think of themselves as having been a part of the Exodus. For Zionists, we were there when Dreyfus was court-martialed.

I loved and respected my father, even though I saw him as weak compared to my mother. He bought and sold furniture in the marketplace

---

3 See Appendix.
4 See Appendix.

in Krakow. I rode with him in his wagon. When I was old enough, he let me handle the reins. He had a habit of lifting his hat when he saw someone he knew. If he had a bad day, he would say business was good when asked. If he had a good day, he would say business wasn't so good. He was modest. He embraced technology by having a phone installed in our home, and when he answered it, he lifted his hat when saying hello. Later, we would drift apart, as did many of my peers, because of Zionist dreams. My father was Orthodox and, like the others, did not support the Zionist movement or socialism. It was troublemaking and had no basis in Jewish thought. Only the Messiah could restore the Jewish people to their land, but my generation was tired of waiting for the Messiah.

At thirteen I became a bar mitzvah and graduated from public school. It was the time when all children of humble backgrounds got a job or, with luck, an apprenticeship. Our neighborhood was mixed, but it was centered around the old Jewish neighborhood, so it was primarily Jewish. I was lucky to become an apprentice at a printing shop outside the Jewish neighborhood in Krakow to a printer who did not care if I was Jewish. He cared about skill, and I was always good with my hands. It was not long before I was more interested in fixing and maintaining the machinery than I was at setting type, and I proved myself valuable.

The word "valuable," it was an important word at work and an even more important word for a Jew living under the Nazis. Leaving the Jewish world and entering the gentile world every day was like a new birth. Jumping on a moving trolley car and looking out at the world was so exhilarating. I could even forget about the chocolate that I could now afford to buy every once in a while.

Every week I dutifully brought home my pay and gave it to my mother, who returned a portion to me. I was becoming a man despite the fact that I still wore knickers and a cap. I was the oldest and needed to help the family. As my voice changed, I developed a strong singing voice. I made extra money as a paid choir member in the main synagogue. Still, I slowly pulled away from that Orthodox Jewish world. Not only did I see factories that I dreamed of someday owning, but I started eating kielbasa. Yes, it was forbidden fruit—greasy, fatty, spicy, delicious pork sausage. It was the stuff that Poles ate every day, and every day I felt more like a Pole. I began to admire the assimilated Jews who lived outside the Jewish section. I could be one of them. Remain Jewish, dress and act like the others, and be part of the modern Polish state where everyone had equal rights. Someday, I would invent something and own a factory where dozens, maybe hundreds, of workers would look to me for their livelihood. When I was eighteen, I would be training on the weekends for the Polish reserves. I would serve my country, and everyone would see that I was no different from the Poles except for my religion. Marshal Pilsudski promised that. He promised equality. He was the father of the nation.

General Josef Pilsudski was always a Polish nationalist. He lived in czarist-controlled Poland. For being a leftist and a nationalist, the czar exiled him to Siberia. In 1914, with the support of the Austrians, he formed a Polish army and fought the Russians. Though he knew that Poland would temporarily end up under the Germans, he believed in an ultimate Allied victory leading to a free Poland. At the end of the war, he did not wait for recognition from the Allies. Instead, he declared an independent Poland and became dictator. He was later elected president. He died in 1935. He beat the Bolsheviks when they tried to reclaim the czarist empire and take away Poland's freedom in 1920. He made us a nation again and built a modern army that could withstand any assault by our historic oppressors, the Germans, the Austrians, and the Russians.

It was a beautiful world that was full of hopes and dreams. I could be an industrialist and, at the same time, dream of being a Zionist, going to Palestine, and building a new world. Nothing was really out of reach, and the coming war was not even worth a thought. I began building and repairing racing bicycles and was soon racing on an indoor track. I took up boxing. I was quick and hit hard. Too bad that I was short and had a hooked Jewish nose sticking out, waiting to be broken. It was no matter, because I was with my Jewish friends whom I grew up with, and we were all full of hope. I was lucky because only a peasant who had so little could dream of something greater, especially at a time when anything seemed possible. Even the Depression did not hit us as hard as the other countries. Germany still needed our resources.

Every day, I went home to a small apartment. At night, we laid down mattresses. Eight of us slept in one room: five children, my parents, and an orphan woman who lived with us and helped my mother. This is what happened to orphans. I considered myself very lucky to have an intact family. I loved my brothers and sisters, especially Halina. She would be the light in a world that would soon grow horribly black.

By the early 1930s, the radio content from Germany started broadcasting anti-Semitic speeches. Over time, the frequency and vitriol increased. Marshal Pilsudski became old and weak and eventually died in 1935. Right-wing parties took over the government. The church's ugly anti-Semitism rose again just when we thought it had been extinguished. Ever since the founding fathers of the church decided that Jews could survive but not thrive, a fertile ground of dehumanization was plowed. It rose and fell like waves, but even in the calmest times, the undercurrent was there. No, the church did not create the Shoah. Instead, it created minds that could somehow accept the fate of the Jews as God's will. The world was getting darker, but there was still hope.

"Hatikvah," which means "the hope," is the anthem of Zionism. The hope was in the flames. The bonfire was lit, and the night was illuminated. There is something about a large fire at night that captures the mind. Perhaps it is in our genes. It burns away the fear that our prehistoric ancestors had, the fear of animals and spirits. The Nazis used it to ignite a twisted, hate-filled idealism in their youth. The Zionists used it to ignite hope in a new world. The Nazis used it inspire fear in their enemies. The Zionists used it to inspire young people to dream of a better world. I fell in love with that dream even as the world around me was becoming hostile.

I became so involved with the Zionist movement that I let go of my other dreams and decided I would go to Palestine to help build a new world. First, I had to learn how to be a farmer so I would be able to work on a kibbutz, which is a communal farm. Building these farms was how we would settle the land. I liked tending the animals and working the fields. Jews were not farmers, but now I was working on a farm, a practice communal farm. I was to become the ideal farmer-intellectual-pioneer and fighter. It was the last step before leaving for Palestine. I was eighteen. The year was 1938. The propaganda against the Jews streamed from the radio. I was ready to commit my life to a cause. At the bonfires we sang folk songs. I felt a part of a special community. Women and men held hands and danced around the fire. The orthodox community was shocked by this behavior, but I was elated by the feeling of liberation. Men and women would be equal. Religion and the ghetto mentality would have no place in our new world. It brought us a sense of hope and idealism that was spiritually liberating. We were infected with enthusiasm. We discussed, we argued: about socialism, communism, God, *Der Judenstadt* (Theodore Herzl's book about building a Jewish homeland in Palestine), whether a war was coming, the young people who went before us and died of malaria draining the swamps, the rightness of our cause, and our absolute right to live in Palestine. We talked of the Bible as history. We memorized the names and the stories. We were ready to join the Haganah, the Jewish underground. We were ready.

My mother was not quite ready. She understood my need, my burning to influence history, to make a new world. But she needed my help. "Stay one more year, Mates," she said. "We need the income and the help. Helen will be sixteen and be able to do more. Just stay one more year." This was my destiny—to lose my dream but to help my family.

Four

LIFE UNDER STALIN: MATES BRUNER

The death of one man is a tragedy.
The death of millions is a statistic.

—JOSEF STALIN

The bright light in my head was starting to fade, and the tears were stopping so I was getting my vision back. All the while, I had been trying to stop the blood from squirting out my nose. It was slowing down now. This was the second time my nose had been broken. The first time put an end to my boxing career. I knew the pain I would have again when I went to the hospital and they straightened it out. What would I tell the doctors? I couldn't tell them the truth. I was scared. I would have to make up some kind of story. I would worry about that later as I rode my bike to the hospital. I couldn't tell them I had taken a shoe and smashed myself in the face. It isn't easy to hit yourself that hard. The first few times were not hard enough. There was no other way out. It was either a broken nose or go to jail. Finally, I just shut my eyes and did it.

I was in Boryslaw,[5] in the Russian zone. This was the home of my father and mother; my grandparents; and my cousins, aunts, and uncles.

---

5 See Appendix.

It was in the Ukrainian part of Poland. My family lived there under the old Austrian Empire. It became part of the new independent Poland at the end of World War I. When my father remarried after the death of his first wife, he moved to Krakow. I had waited too long to go to Palestine. It was the price I paid for being a good son and helping out the family. When the war came to Poland, my mother decided I really couldn't help out anymore under the Nazis. There was no work. My father had been processed already. He shaved his beard and went to the processing center with all his papers, including his bank accounts. The center was a long building with a long counter, like a bank. At each window, there was a bureaucrat instead of a bank teller. My father moved from window to window. When he started, he was a Polish citizen. By the time he got to the last window, he was a penniless, stateless Jew and an enemy of the German fatherland.

When the war started in September 1939, I waited to be called up to the reserves. I had been going to the shooting range on weekends and was taught to drill. I did not want to fight. It wasn't in my plans to be a hero for Poland, but as long as there was no choice, I would do my duty like my uncle Isaac had for Austria in World War I.

My uncle Isaac was drafted in World War I. Although there was no official or government sponsored anti-Semitism in Austria, there was a strong undercurrent in Austria and the other nations in its empire. After all, it was in Vienna where Hitler first developed his anti-Jewish beliefs. As in all nations where the Jews lived, they joined the army and fought in their country's wars.

There are two good stories about his service, both as a new recruit. The Austrian army was as out of date as the Russian army, and corporal punishment was the norm. As a new recruit, my uncle was placed in a barracks with other new recruits; there was one difference: he was a Jew. No one called him by his name. They just referred to him as Jew. He was voted as the one who would have to get up early and make coffee for the others. Every morning when he got up early, he found shit in his boots. He said nothing. He cleaned out his boots and made the coffee. The other recruits said nothing. They just smiled at him and said, "You make really good coffee, Jew." One night, after a few weeks of this, he lay in his bunk after the lights went out, and he heard someone yell, "Hey, Jew, how do you like having shit in your boots?" The uncontrollable laughter went around the barracks.

Uncle Isaac waited for the laughter to die down. When everyone stopped laughing, he said in a very calm voice, "If you stop shitting in my boots, then I promise I will stop pissing in your coffee." Everyone got quiet. The next morning his boots were clean. No one mentioned whether the coffee tasted any different, but now they knew why Isaac did not drink coffee in the morning.

The weeks of hard training went on. Uncle Isaac got up early to make the coffee. Then he went to his footlocker and got out his tallit, tefillin, yarmulke, and prayer book. He faced the wall because that was the eastern direction, and he quietly said his prayers. When he was done, he carefully folded his tallit, wrapped up his tefillin, and neatly stowed his things in his footlocker just as the men were being called to order.

Near the end of training, there was a surprise inspection. The sergeant came in with an officer to show off his troops who were about to graduate. The officer was a gray-haired colonel with an immaculate uniform, beard, and fluffy sideburns. All the soldiers jumped from their bunks, got dressed, and stood at attention. All except Uncle Isaac. He was in the middle of his prayers. The sergeant called to him, but he did not answer. He went on with his prayers while the sergeant and colonel waited by his bunk, looking at Isaac's back. When he was done, he folded his tallit, wrapped his tefillin, and neatly stowed his things in his footlocker. Then he calmly stepped up to the front of his bunk and stood at attention. The sergeant's face could not have been redder, and the recruits could not help but snicker at him. Yes, the Jew would finally get what was coming to him. He would be flogged and maybe go to prison. Isaac was unfazed. He had been praying every morning since he could remember, and no matter what happened, he would do the same again. Before the sergeant could open his mouth, the colonel pointed his finger at Isaac and spoke up. "Everyone should take a lesson from this man. He knows who he is, he knows his duty, and he will perform it regardless of the consequences." The colonel walked on by.

I never got the chance to be called up. The Poles were the first to face a new kind of war called "blitzkrieg." They were ordered to retreat to the east, where they could form a denser, more defensible line. As they were forming up for their last stand against the Germans, the Russians invaded from the east. Poland was partitioned. Its short-lived rebirth of independence was over.

"There is nothing you can do here, Mates," my mother said. "You are nineteen; you can take care of yourself. We need to stay here with the younger children. We cannot smuggle the family to the Russian zone. You need to save yourself." My father agreed with her. As we packed my rucksack, my father took a tallit, tefillin, a yarmulke, and a prayer book and put them in my pack. My mother took them back out. "He doesn't need them now. It won't help him, and he doesn't have much room. Better he should take some extra food," she said to my father. The tears welled up in both their eyes. The family was starting to break up. I wanted to help them, but my mother was right; there was nothing I could do. There wasn't much food, and no one knew what the Nazis would do next. If I could get to the Russian zone, I could work and send food. I took off my armband with the yellow star and headed down the road. If the Germans stopped me, I would be shot. Things had already gotten to the point where people were taking chances with their lives. After a while, you just got used to it. Who knew if you would be alive tomorrow, even if you didn't break the rules?

I traveled at night and slept in the woods during the day. I dared not show my face to anyone. You never knew when a Pole would point you out to the Germans to win their favor. I ceased being Polish the day the Germans invaded. I made my way east to the San River, the dividing line between the Russian and German zones. I went into the river, but the current was strong, and the river twisted around several bends. When I got to the bank, I did not know which side I was on. I waited in the tall

grasses, not knowing what to do until I heard the voices of Russian sol-
diers looking for those who had crossed the river. They gave me a ride to
Boryslaw. They did not seem to care that I was a Jew, though they did call
me "Abramchik." I had heard that Lenin said anti-Semitism was as bad as
being a counterrevolutionary. That may have been true in Lenin's time.
Lenin was an internationalist, and so was Trotsky. Stalin was a Slavophile.
As we all knew, the Slavophiles had won out against the internationalists.
Trotsky was a Jew. Stalin killed Trotsky, and in Stalin's paranoid mind, all
Jewish communists were suspect. It was a confusing time. To the Nazis,
the Jews were all Bolsheviks, but they were also greedy capitalists. To the
Soviets, the Jews were internationalists. For me, I was no longer part of
any "ik," "ism," or "ist." I was a survivalist, and it was a one-man show.

Once the Russians became allies with the West, Stalin let all nationalities within the Soviet empire flourish—anything to push patriotism for
the motherland: religion, nationalism, and the prerevolutionary arts. He
encouraged Yiddish culture. He sponsored Yiddish poets, playwrights,
and musicians. Of course, once the war was over, it was off to the gulags.
Religion was once again the opium of the masses, and regional nationalism was to be crushed.

For now, things were good. They gave me a job on an oil-drilling
rig. I worked with engineers who taught me drafting at night. There
was an opportunity after working with the engineers that I could go to
school. I liked the preciseness of the engineers, and I enjoyed learning
draftsmanship. My newest goal was to become an engineer. The Russians
could be a very warm people. They would give you the shirt off their
backs if they liked you, and they seemed to like me. They liked vodka;
they liked a good joke—the dirtier the better—and a hearty slap on the
back. They liked all women—the bigger the better—and they could easily break into a song and dance.

They had a dark side, though. They were used to killing and being killed. If they did not like you, it was time to run. Their soldiers
liberated camps and helped the prisoners. They could also go into a
frenzy of drinking and raping. Only the Russian soldiers raped female

concentration camp survivors who hardly looked like women and were covered with lice.

It was a completely peasant society. Stalin had killed most of the officers from the revolution. He killed the intelligentsia, teachers, doctors, lawyers, middle-class farmers, and former business owners. What little trust he had, he put in the peasants. Only Stalin could make a peasant into an engineer or raise a coal miner to an army officer or even a general, and many loved him for it. When you were with them, you had to be just as jolly and just as crude. You had to be a comrade. Any sign of refinement or revulsion was a bourgeois mannerism and made you suspect as a counterrevolutionary.

They also had their rules, and being late for work would land you in prison. When my alarm clock stopped working during the night, and I overslept, what could I do? I broke my nose, stomped on my bike, walked to the hospital, and told them I had an accident on my way to work. Once I had the doctor's note, I was in the clear. A broken nose was a small price for staying out of prison.

I tried to send packages home as often as I could. No matter how good I had it, I was always worried about my parents. The Nazis had set up a ghetto outside Krakow. They also allowed Jews to settle in villages outside of Krakow. My parents went to a town called Slomniki. They believed it was safer and healthier for the children than being in the ghetto. We wrote to one another often. When I could scratch enough extra money and rations together, I would get food and send it to them. There were things I could get that they could not, like sugar, coffee, flour, and, of course, chocolate. I had to go to the post office in Lvov, about 120 kilometers from Boryslaw.

I had come to Boryslaw in November of 1939. Even if the Germans did turn on Russia, we were assured of the strength, bravery, and power of the Soviet army. Of course, they could not explain their failure in Finland, and I am sure Hitler saw it as proof that the Soviets were not as powerful as they thought. The Slavic people were sub-humans or *untermenschen* to the Nazis. They did not enjoy the same right to the eastern lands as the German people. It wasn't just about war; the East had to be depopulated.

The Germans invaded in late June 1941. As they did in Poland, they came in like lightning. Stalin, the only leader as devious as Hitler, was actually shocked that the Germans broke the Molotov-Ribbentrop[6] pact. He helped the Germans. He was sure the reports of a German attack were a mistake. He ordered his men not to fight at first. He needed confirmation from those he trusted before ordering his men to fight. He did not want to provoke the Germans. He helped the Germans because he had killed most of the experienced officers in his army before the war. He helped them because of his brutal, murderous repression of the nations in his empire, especially the Ukrainians. When the Germans invaded, the people of the Baltic republics threw flowers at the soldiers. No one could believe there could be a worse ruler than Stalin. They would learn soon enough that this was a mistake when the SS Einsatzkommandos and Einsatzgruppen came in and started their mass murders. They did not mind too much when it involved the Jews and communist party members, but it soon turned against all the intelligentsia. In the Ukraine and Lithuania, a nationalist party allied itself with the Germans. They formed an army and fought with the Germans. They helped eliminate Jews and served as guards in the ghettos and concentration camps.

I was in Lvov at the post office the day the war started. It was late June, and by early July, they had taken the region. I tried to move east, but I could not move fast enough. Despite my mother's efforts, the Germans got hold of me, too. Life was about to get worse for tens of millions of people, as though it weren't already bad enough. Jewish refugees were ordered to return to their hometowns. My hometown was Krakow, but my immediate family now lived in the village of Slomniki. I had no permission to go there, but I had to see my family. I had to know how my parents, my brother, and my three sisters were doing. I had to see Sabina, the youngest. She was only seven years old now. I missed her and wondered how she was being affected. I knew my brother Laser,

---

6 See Appendix.

now eleven, would be helping the family. He might get some ideas of protecting them from the German soldiers. I needed to talk to him and tell him not to do anything crazy. I wanted to see Halina, who was now twelve. She was a sweet, happy girl. I missed her smile very much. Helen was about sixteen now. She had come to Boryslaw a few months after me but left within a year because she missed the family so much. She was always strong willed. She butted heads with me a lot, but I still loved her as much as anyone.

I was ready to take a risk. I bribed a low-ranking German officer to smuggle me as close as he could to Slomniki. I could have been shot just for asking. The officer helped me. He told me to get on the roof of a truck and lie flat. The truck got me close to Slomniki. I was not wearing my armband. I walked along the road as though I had nothing to fear. Soon I was in the town and home with my family. I could not stay long. I had already taken a great risk.

Five

MY OTHER FATHER: SAM BRUNER

When we were young, our family had little
We shared a small room and bed
It was the symbol of how close we became

You helped me, protected me, taught me
You helped raise me and supported me
We shared music and drinks, dreams of the future, and
Playboy *magazines*

I chased after you, big brother
As little boys looking for a hero will do
I made the right choice in the person I chased
Because you were a man worth looking up to

—SAM BRUNER

B ill Cosby was a young comedian. We saved our money so we could buy his records and listen to them over and over until we memorized his routines. He called his father the "giant." He said his parents' bedroom was downstairs, and his room was upstairs. When his father came home and needed to see him (probably because he did something wrong), he could hear the giant's footsteps coming up the stairs. He knew it was the giant because the sound was louder than anyone else's. "The giant is coming up the stairs," he would say in a deep voice.

We lived in a small, Cape-style house. The downstairs had two small bedrooms, one for my parents and one for my sister. We had a large bedroom upstairs. Harry, Joe, and I slept there. When my father climbed the stairs, we said the giant was coming. We never knew if we were in trouble. We could hear the giant's footsteps and waited to see what would happen.

By sixth grade, Joe had gotten into the habit of not doing homework if he did not care for the subject. He did not care about Hebrew school at all and thought it was a waste of time. It is not that the rest of us thought there was any value in it, but we did do our homework so we wouldn't get in trouble. Joe was the only kid I knew who actually had to repeat a year of Hebrew school. I knew kids who never learned one Hebrew letter and did their whole bar mitzvah by having the cantor write out everything in English letters. How much worse could Joe have been? Perhaps because he had a *Mad Magazine* open on top of his Hebrew book in class. Maybe it was when he got caught with the hollowed-out book that had the transistor radio in it and the earphone cable coming up his sleeve.

Joe also stopped doing homework in public school when he did not like the subject. If he liked it, he got an A. If he didn't, he would fail the subject. His teacher, Mrs. Krauss, and his Hebrew schoolteacher, Mr. Bender (we called him Bagel Bender), started sending home notes on a regular basis. My father threatened Joe in many ways, but he did not respond. You could move a mountain easier than you could move Joe if he did not want to do something. Even if you put dynamite under his bottom, he would not move. At least that is what my mother would say. My father was not fond of that attitude. He demanded respect. He was master of the house, and disobedience showed a lack of respect.

Finally, the night came. We heard the footsteps of the giant. He flipped on the light. He had his belt in his hand. He stepped into the room and said to Joe that another note came home today. Joe said nothing. Joe got out of bed wearing only his underpants. He walked up to my father and turned his back to him.

My father said, "What are you doing?"

"Well, you're going to whip me, aren't you?"

"You bet I am," my father said in an enraged voice and proceeded to whip Joe's back and legs with the belt.

Joe yelled in pain but he never moved. He never cried, not then, and I never did see him cry at any other time in his life. Joe was covered in large red welts. In his own way, he had beaten Dad. Joe never gave in. Dad took his toys, his money, and tried everything else. He never hit him again, though.

I watched this scene when I was eight years old. I knew that no matter how old I got, I would never have done what Joe did. There were some things about him that would take decades to understand. I would not call it courage. I would say he had a level of defiance that was quiet, and he would not let pain get in the way. It was not as horrifying as seeing my mother beaten, but it was still pretty shocking.

Joe stood up for all of us, in a way. We might still get an occasional slap in the face or a backhand to the head, but never as hard as he used to. I guess he realized it was no use.

Now, Gena was Dad's little princess. He always had a smile for her. She would ask him for a dime to get an ice cream cone. He was always giving her sweets. I would never ask my father because I knew he would put me to work first. I had my mother. She would always give me that dime. She could never hit me hard, no matter how mad she was. She would wind up and swing, but would pull it, and by the time her hand hit my cheek, I could barely feel it. If my mother wanted to punish me, she just had to let me know how disappointed she was. That was enough to make me cry.

I cannot remember my father hitting Gena. Maybe he did, but at least not often enough that I could remember. He had other ways for dealing with his princess. Gena didn't like to clean up her room. My father had a problem with girls who were not neat and tidy. It didn't fit in to his idea of what a little girl should be. One day, after warning her several times, he came into her room and cut off the heads of her dolls. Gena kept a pretty clean room after that.

I will give my father credit for a few things. He could have deserted us. We would have had no support. My mother would not be able to raise four children alone, and she had no backup. The family was just too small and spread too far apart. The war saw to that. My mother could not provide the discipline. Though Dad was harsh, he did keep us in line and out of a lot of trouble. He could have been a drunk or a gambler. He could have been a more serious abuser. I saw kids in school with black eyes and broken arms. He wanted us to be productive and successful, though he had his own ideas about what that success was.

He did do one thing that I will always be grateful for. He made me read books. He didn't pick the books, but we both liked biographies. Because he and my mother worked so much, we were alone in the house more than other children we knew. That meant we were watching too much TV. My father told me to get a book out of the library, read it, and give him an oral report, and he would give me two dollars. My allowance at the time was twenty-five cents a week. Minimum wage probably wasn't that high, and I was only in third or fourth grade. I started reading with a passion: history and biographies. After a few books, I was reading so fast that I couldn't be bothered trying to pin my father down to give him the report.

Joe also read a lot and encouraged me. He liked being my big brother. Harry was good to me, but he was six years older. Gena was my playmate, but she was a girl, after all, and our games were not the same. Joe was four years older, and we had a better connection. Sure, he pushed me around and teased me, but so did my other siblings. I was the youngest, after all. That just sharpened my wit and sarcasm. It was the only weapon I had. I may have gotten hit for it, but as least I knew I got my shot in.

Joe encouraged me to read nonfiction because that would make me really smart. He showed me how to use the encyclopedia. He would make me look things up when I had a question. We didn't have much money when we were little, but Dad insisted on having an encyclopedia in the house, even if he could not read English very well. He knew it was important for the children.

Joe was an artist. We built model airplanes and battleships together. Mine were pretty sloppy. His were perfect. He liked to teach. He showed me how to put the glue on the inside of the seam and use a razor blade to cut away the plastic flash and paint the parts first. Eventually we built just about every fighter plane and bomber that was used in World War II. We also built an X-15 (the first rocket ship to reach the edge of space). Finally, we built a Mercury spaceship because John Glenn was one of our heroes. We both had the same ambition: to join the air force and fly fighter planes. Perhaps we could become astronauts or join the Israeli air force, because they were still doing close-range dogfighting.

By the fourth grade, I needed glasses, which squelched my dream. Joe developed a rare disease at the time called ileitis, which would be the cause of his early death. Both of us were out of the air force. We took our planes, heated up a metal rod over the stove, melted holes in the fuselages, shoved firecrackers inside, lit them, and threw them in the air to watch them explode. Another American plane lost to a Zero or a Messerschmitt. The ships were put into the old backyard baby pool, doused with lighter fluid, and attacked by a firecracker-laden kamikaze plane.

My father was always busy. Joe showed me how to tie my sneakers so the strings wouldn't come loose. He showed me how to throw, catch, and hit a baseball. He taught me how to swim. He taught me how to tune up my first car.

I glorified him until the day I found him cheating. We had lots of those little army men. The green ones were Americans. The blue-green were the Germans, and the yellow ones were the Japanese. We would build forts with shoes, boxes, and other toys. We would each take a turn firing at the other's fort, using the old Mattel rifles that shot pointed plastic bullets and my Mighty Mo cannon. Both were really dangerous toys by today's standards. Joe easily knocked down my forts and shot my men. He was always winning. Finally, I found out that he was using scotch tape to hold his things down. I never played that game with him again. I knew if I started using tape, he would probably start nailing things down.

As we got older, sharing a bedroom in the night and waiting for sleep with the lights out, he would tell me the mysterious secrets of girls, sex, and urban legends. In my sophomore year of college, I rented my first apartment. Joe insisted he help set me up. We drove down to West Virginia. He brought all his old stuff from his past apartments. He showed me how to bake a chicken, make spaghetti using plenty of cheap wine, and a few other basic dishes. Not only was he showing me survival skills, he wanted to make sure I could invite a girl over and impress her by making dinner. He felt that teaching me how to get laid was an important part of his tutelage. We went to the bank to set up my first checking account. While I was filling out paperwork, he left and came back later with scented candles. It was then that he shared his complete formula for getting laid. Make dinner, serve plenty of cheap wine, turn down the lights, and put out scented candles. He told me the candles created shadows and softened up the features. Between the wine and the candles, we would both look more attractive than we really were.

I was fifty-seven years old when Joe died, less than a year after I moved to Atlanta. I was visiting Philadelphia the day before Joe died. I stopped by the store to shoot the breeze. After over thirty years of working together, I had left the business. In all those years, we had plenty of disagreements. Many became quite personal, and working together all week meant very little socializing on weekends. However, in all those years, we never argued about money. We trusted each other implicitly, and there was never an action on either side that ever raised a suspicion.

Four years earlier, I announced I would be changing careers and going to law school at night. Joe knew it had been an earlier dream of mine that my father had squelched. The time had come for a change, and Joe knew it, but he did not like it. He gave me a pretty hard time over those four years. I didn't want to fight with him. We had been together too long, and I knew that running the business alone would be a hardship. I loved him too much to have it end badly. Like a father, though, while he may have disapproved, I would find out later that he was bragging about me. After I took my last exam, he finally congratulated me. I had no idea until I had to liquidate his business and contact the customers just how much he was bragging about my passing the bar and landing a job. One customer after another said the same thing: "You have no idea how proud he was of you."

Joe was Dad's favorite in many ways. Unfortunately, Dad did play favorites. Dad was good with his hands. It was his mechanical skills that helped him survive the war. He was "valuable" to the Germans. To be "smart" in Dad's view, you had to have a certain common sense that he believed was necessary to fix things or be a mechanic. Joe was the best of us. I was sufficient. Harry wasn't very good. He was also missing a bit of common sense in my father's eyes, and so my father often told him that he was "stupid." It is not that Harry wasn't good in school. He did very well, especially in the sciences, and eventually became a pharmacist. As far as my father was concerned, not many days would go by without Harry being told just how stupid he was.

After that last meeting with Joe, I walked to my car and thought about when I was a teenager. Joe's friends never seemed to care that I was four years younger. Joe took me along with his friends to lots of places. That day, I was thinking about when I was fifteen. It was a Sunday. Joe said he was meeting up with some of his biking friends and going to the drag races at the Atco speedway in New Jersey. He liked giving me rides on his motorcycle. He would often give me a ride to junior high school. We would pass the school bus on the way. He would come screeching into the parking lot, let me off, and do a wheelie on his way out of the parking lot. It was a pretty cool way to show up at school, and Joe wanted to make sure his little brother was cool.

Speeding down the back roads of New Jersey, my long hair blowing in the wind, the wind on my face making it feel numb, and the smells of rivers and farms were all part of the thrill of riding with a pack. What nineteen-year-old would take his fifteen-year-old brother along with a motorcycle pack? I didn't know anyone else like that.

While Joe was preparing for the drag race, I walked around. I ate the greasy hot dogs, smoked cigarettes, smelled the gasoline and exhaust, and watched some big, mean-looking gang members tend to their Harley Hogs. They did not have electric starters then. To start those bikes you had to be big. You had to jump up and come down with your body weight on the kick-starter. I knew my friends were not having a Sunday like this, because they did not have big brothers like this. We rode home late in the day. The other bikers peeled off toward their homes.

The pack became smaller as we rode along. We rode over the Walt Whitman Bridge late in the day. I could see the river and the ships and smell the refineries. We rode through the old inner-ring suburb of Darby that used to be filled with factories, providing a solid base of blue-collar workers. Those old factories were going out one by one. Darby was decaying like the other inner-ring suburbs; the first ones built that butted up against the border of Philadelphia. They were full of row homes built for families who became part of the first wave of the exodus from the city. We kept riding to our home in Secane, a split-level on a street where all the split-levels looked the same. Inside, my mother would be cooking as always. Dinner would be good, usually meat and potatoes. Dad would probably be pleasant unless we started talking about Vietnam. We would watch *60 Minutes* together and probably play a game of chess. Life was good at that moment.

The day after visiting Joe in the store, I found Joe lying facedown on his bedroom floor. The state policeman said he was dead. I yelled at Joe to get up. The EMT also said he was gone. I asked how he knew. He reached down and touched him and said he was cold. I bent down and touched him. He was cold. I called my wife, Deb, and yelled that it can't be. He can't be dead. Not Joe. *What about the business?* I thought. *What will I tell his sons?* "Hi, Dan. Guess what I found on the floor of your dad's house today?" "Hey, Marc. How is your day going? Mine isn't going so well." What about my mother? Joe was driving forty-five minutes up to the life-care facility after work and on weekends every time my mother called, no matter how small the issue. He was buying half a dozen kosher chickens a week so my mother could make the soup for my father after he came home from dialysis. Harry was in Boston. I did not feel guilty for living in Atlanta only because I knew Joe would be looking after my parents. He called me to discuss every decision he needed to make regarding my parents. Gena and my father were so estranged that she was not around to help.

Her "Joey" was the child my mother worried about the most when we were young. He was very sick from age thirteen on. She left work early to take a bus up to Children's Hospital in North Philadelphia, already a dangerous area. She waited for the bus home at eleven at night, in the dark, in a frightening neighborhood, and the doctors could tell her nothing. All they could do was perform exploratory surgery and remove bits and pieces of his small intestine. Her other children were home making their own dinners, and she felt guilty about that. She always had a hard life. When a parent has to worry about one child more than the others, it creates a special bond. She always worried about Joe. She brought chicken soup to the store for decades to make sure Joe wasn't eating junk after he was divorced and working all those hours.

How on earth could I explain this to her in a way that she could understand, now that she was so easily confused and concerned for my father's health? It wasn't fair, and his death wasn't comprehensible.

A crowd of neighbors had gathered. The state policeman decided to play Kojak (a famous TV detective) while I was obviously in shock. He wanted to know whether, given the economic circumstances, Joe could have committed suicide. "No," I said with a smile. Joe thought much too highly of himself to commit suicide. Other than during his first divorce, I never saw him depressed. He was stoic. He was the one who stood there and took the beating for all of us. Like my father, he could be very controlling. He struggled during his life. He struggled with his disease and tried to never let it get him down. He struggled to raise his children with some sense of order. He struggled with his two wives to make them more subservient. He struggled to be perfect when crafting a piece of jewelry for a customer.

Kojak kept going. He wanted to know whether, as partners, with the bad economy, there were any disagreements about money between us. I told him I'd left the business and moved to Atlanta eight months before. Besides, we never argued about money. He still wanted to know if he owed me money. At this point I was becoming obviously agitated, so Kojak proceeded to question Deb, who had come over to the house by then.

Eventually Kojak left. The assistant coroner took Joe to the morgue for an autopsy. The neighbors dispersed. Deb wanted to comfort me, but there was nothing she could say or do. I sat down, dizzy. I looked around the living and dining room. I saw sculptures he made, photographs and memorabilia from growing up. I saw clocks everywhere. We had both collected antique clocks. I remembered every transaction from every clock. I knew each one's history, when it was bought, and why we decided who would bring it home. My eyes went faster and faster around the room, and then I had to think about the business and what to tell my nephews. Finally, the primal scream came. He was gone. The coroner would let me know that he was the victim of almost fifty years of steroid use to control his ileitis. My brother, my friend, my confidant, the one person who stood with me against my father was gone. I had lost the father who meant the most to me.

Six

Plaszow: Mates Bruner

From hell's heart I stab at thee;
for hate's sake, I spit my last breath at thee.

—Herman Melville, *Moby-Dick*

The horrid stench still comes to my nose, no matter how old I get. The heat of summer 1944 made it worse. Once again I curled my index finger and shoved it into my mouth so I would not scream. I thought the screaming was over. I thought I had seen enough death. They liquidated Russian prisoners here. The Russian army was getting close, so we had to dig up the bodies and burn them. As we dug, the ashes came down like snow. Wood was laid down first. The rotted corpses were piled like cordwood on top, doused with gasoline, and left to burn. It would not be the last of the corpses I would have to burn in this war. Later it would be Germans. That would not be quite so hard.

You may have seen or read *Schindler's List,* but no movie or book can describe the horror of Plaszow. No actor in any movie where people are starving can get thin enough, dirty enough, smelly enough, louse-infected enough; sick enough with dysentery, TB, or typhus; or just plain wretched enough and still able to work a twelve-hour day in the lime pit.

Lime—it was the same stuff that had burned my eyes as a child. Here it burned my eyes, my lungs, my throat, my nose, and my skin. No one can truly imagine the horror, the sadism, or the degradation until you have lived it. The only good thing you could say about Plaszow is that there were worse places you could end up. Plaszow was a relatively safe place for Jews. It was hell on earth for Russian POWs. Russians were good for only one thing: slave labor at rations that would ensure their quick death. The Jews could wait a little. There were untold millions of Russians, and Western Russia was to be depopulated so that Germany could have its lebensraum.[7]

I left Slomniki for the ghetto in Krakow. Later my mother would send Helen. My mother was still trying to spread the family around, spread the risk. She would pack Helen a bag, make her take off her star, and get a bus to the city. Helen went out on the road, cried, and never saw her parents or Sabina and Laser again—and neither would I. My poor mother was watching the family pull apart, one by one. Helen and I were together in the ghetto for a short time.

Plaszow was first opened in 1940 as a forced labor camp for Poles, with Ukrainian guards. In 1941 the SS came, and the camp was enlarged to become a concentration camp. They needed room for Russian prisoners and Jewish workers. The commandant was Hanz Müller. I volunteered to help with the expansion. Helping to enlarge the camp meant increased rations. It also meant working outside of the dank, fetid air of the ghetto. It was orderly, and I had become used to brutality and short rations. It was obvious that the ghettos and villages that housed the Jews would eventually be liquidated and the Jews concentrated in camps as they had already been in Germany. We would all end up here or in some other camp. Better in a forced labor camp where the food was at a minimally acceptable amount, and we were not being exterminated. Nazi doctors had carefully calculated the rations so that we would slowly die as we worked. The Nazis would have their labor and eliminate us at the same time. They never expected that our bodies would adjust.

---

7 See Appendix.

From Hell's Heart

Men would stop growing beards. Women would stop menstruating. Our nonessential body functions would shut down, and we would survive on these lower rations. This is why the Nazis needed a "final solution." We could survive here. I never picked up a piece of food that fell to the ground, no matter how hungry I was, and there would be times I would be driven nearly to madness with hunger. I never drank milk or ate a piece of meat given to me by the Nazis, and I never got dysentery. I only ate the vegetables, butter, and bread. I scraped my nails on rocks to keep them short so they could not collect dirt. I got up early every morning and washed my body in cold water and used soap. The time of year did not matter. I did not care if there was snow on the ground. If I did not have soap, I traded for it as desperately as a piece of food, even if the penalty was death.

I remembered the hospital I was in as a boy and how clean it was. To me, soap and clean food gave me a chance at life. I believed with all my heart that I would make it somehow. I do not know why, but I had a burning belief that I was destined to survive and find my family. I saw so many others who had lost their will. They were afraid to break the rules. They gave up. This was their destiny, but it would not be mine. As the months went by, it became harder and harder.

I had promised Helen that I would find a way to get her into the camp. I would bribe someone. You could always bribe someone. Trade some bread for cigarettes. Trade some cigarettes for kielbasa. Trade some kielbasa for a bottle of wine. I could not get Helen into the camp, though. She had already been classified as not being valuable. There was that word again. It was a hard word to get around. I did everything I could, but I failed in this effort. When I failed Helen, I also knew I was failing my mother.

I became used to the risks as long as they were taken for the right reason, and that reason was survival. Some people had no control. They ate all the bread. They smoked the cigarettes, and they drank the wine. These things existed to bribe someone for something you needed. To be caught giving a bribe would mean death, but what if not giving the bribe would mean death? What good was the momentary comfort of a bottle of wine if you would go to work in the quarry, and a Nazi would point a gun at you and tell you to jump? These jumpers were called "parachutists." Why give these bastards such pleasure? You would either die in the jump or break a bone and be as good as dead, and they would have a good laugh. I would rather risk the bribe to get out of such work. I got used to the bribing. I was proud of it. I became so cool at risking my life that no Nazi ever suspected I carried contraband.

As important as food and soap was information. As the war progressed, I was consumed by the desire for information. I wanted to know where the Allies were and how long it would to be until we were liberated. Getting this information or spreading it was a shooting offense. When I heard about the German reversals in Russia and that America had joined the war, I knew it was only a matter of time, and I wanted to know how much time I would need to live through this hell and survive. I was no student of history, but how smart did you have to be to know that Germany could not survive a war on two fronts?

I could not avoid all the brutality and sadism, just enough not to die. One day the guards told us to move a tree. We had no tools. They took eight of us and told us to pull it out of the ground. We pushed the tree back and forth for hours to loosen it in the ground. We heaved with all our strength. The guards laughed. They told us we were lazy Jews. They hit us with truncheons while we worked. They struck me across the back many times. Each time it was so hard, I wanted to give up and fall down and let them shoot me. We finally heaved the tree up from the ground. They chose four of us to carry it. The end with the roots was far heavier. I was on that end. I finally collapsed. The tree came down on top of me, and the roots gave just enough cushioning so that I was not crushed. I could not believe I was alive, but I was. I was sure my back was broken, but it wasn't. However, my back was never the same. The guards had a good laugh. I got up, and they let me go. They thought I was a lucky Jew. They were sure I had died under that tree.

How did this happen? How did I become an animal? I was less than an animal. The Nazis did not torture animals. What kind of world was I in, where I had become a toy for spoiled children? They played with me. If I became broken, they would just throw me out with the trash.

The Allied bombings were the most exciting time in any of the camps I was in. We looked up and prayed that the camps would be bombed, even if it meant our own lives would be sacrificed. The underground would spread leaflets, and the Russians, British, and Americans would drop them from bombers. If they saw you pick one up, you would be shot. The threat became so common they might as well have told me I would be locked up for a day or two. I reached out and picked up the leaflets. I put them in my shirt and studied the maps showing the battle lines. There was no mistake about it. After Kursk, the Germans were on the retreat, and the Russians were on the offensive. When I heard about the Normandy invasion, I took it personally. I believed they were coming for me.

I was working in the vegetable garden when I heard a gunshot. A man near me fell to the ground. Later, another shot rang out, and another person fell to the ground. I just kept on working. This was the work of someone new. It was not quite two years until a new commandant, Amon Göth, was assigned, from February 1943 until his arrest in September 1944 for selling supplies meant for the camp, including rations meant to keep slave laborers alive. He also sold off the jewelry and valuables of prisoners and pocketed the money. This money belonged to the Reich and was needed to help pay for the war. The prisoners also belonged to the Reich and had a value based on their contribution of labor.

Of all the Nazis I came in contact with, he was the most sadistic, psychotic criminal I met. Other Nazis who killed did so under rules and guidelines—not that it helped the dead, but it meant the number could not be exceeded or done arbitrarily, provided the prisoner had not broken some rule, or the killing was done to maintain order. Göth killed for the fun of it. He would stand on his porch with a scoped rifle and shoot at prisoners. He would dress up in a white SS uniform, ride on a white horse around the camp and shoot prisoners for his own pleasure.

Things were becoming arbitrary, and the food was becoming less and less. Bribes alone would not keep me alive at this point. I needed a new strategy. I needed to become more valuable.

Every so often, an officer would come into the barracks and ask if there were any watchmakers. Watchmakers were valuable. Armies ran on time, and watches needed fixing. Those who raised their hands were taken out and given a bench in a building. They consumed fewer calories and received increased rations. I asked the watchmakers in the barracks to teach me. There was no hands-on training, but they explained the parts, how they worked, and the theory involved.

One day an officer came to the barracks and asked for a watchmaker. No one raised his hand, so I did. This was a dangerous gamble.

Many years later, I would teach my sons, Joe and Sam, the art of watchmaking. They broke their first watches. It was almost inevitable. The work was too fine, and it took time to develop the dexterity and fine feeling in one's hands. I had no such luxury. I had to make my own tools. I took nails and honed screwdriver tips on a stone. I took two nails and heated the ends and pounded them together. Then I honed fine round tips and made tweezers. The tools were crude. Many other tools were needed, but I had to do without. We did not have proper cleaning fluids. We had to use benzene that left a residue on the parts, making them "sticky."

I sat down at the bench the first day. Göth himself walked over to me and gave me a lady's watch. The parts were much smaller, finer, and more delicate than on a man's watch. Göth said to me, "If this watch does not work, you will die a hero's death." It was the most challenging incentive program I would ever have. I worked slowly and carefully. When it was finished, I gave the watch a shake. I listened for the ticking sound and whether the ticking was even or "in beat." My heart was pounding in my head, and I could not hear it. I asked the watchmaker next to me if he would listen to it. He told me he wanted no part of it.

I handed in the watch. It worked, and I was now an official watchmaker and an extravaluable prisoner. Watchmaking would save my life many times and get me most of the way through the nightmare.

Later on in the war, I would spend some time at Sachsenhausen, near Berlin. The watchmaking shop was set up in a section of the hospital for wounded soldiers. One day an officer came to us and told us there would be an inspection of the hospital, so we had to work in the fields for a few days until the inspection was over. While we were working, the hospital was bombed in the very area where we would have been working. It was one of the many miracles that were needed to survive. I prided myself on how clever I had become, but more than cleverness was needed.

I had lost faith in God. I saw no evidence of God in the camps. If God cared about me, he would have made me a milk cow. I would have been treated much better. I did, however, believe in miracles and destiny. Each new miracle made me more convinced that I was destined to survive another day. Surviving the war was too big a task. Surviving the day was the first job. Sometimes surviving the next few minutes would be enough to get me through the day. From days to weeks and from weeks to months is how I survived. Some people lost track of time, just as they lost track of all hope. I had more than hope. I had faith in my destiny. If I only knew how long it would take for the war to end, my faith would be complete. I could break the years down into months, the months into weeks, and the weeks into days. Concentrating on the days would get me through.

Because he was under investigation by the Gestapo, Göth had no choice but to hire us out like other prisoners and pay the higher-ups for our work. He had also received orders to end the arbitrary killings and account for any prisoners killed. That did not mean that we couldn't be killed. There just had to be some kind of reason for it.

It was a joyous day when Halina came to the camp with news that the family was still alive. Halina was about twelve or thirteen years old now. She told me the latest news. The rumors were that the ghettos and villages were being emptied of Jews, and they would be sent to camps.

The Nazis had decided on a final solution at the Wannsee conference in late 1942. Starvation was not working as quickly as anticipated. The Jews had adapted and did not die fast enough. She told me the villages around Krakow were being emptied of their Jewish populations and that Slomniki would be emptied very soon. My mother had to make a terrible choice: send Halina to Plaszow or keep her with the family and take their chances in another camp. The stories of the extermination camps were leaking out, Auschwitz, Belzec, Chelmno, Maidanek, Sobibor, and Treblinka. These are names that should be imprinted in the mind of every Jew. Almost four million of the approximately six million Jews who died under the Nazis died in these six camps. Almost half of those died in Auschwitz.

My parents wisely guessed that two old people and two young children would probably end up in one of these camps. If Halina was lucky, she might survive in a labor camp. What kind of choice did my parents have to make? How much would my mother have to suffer by sending three children to a concentration camp as the best alternative? It was the kind of choice many mothers and fathers would have to make during the war. Essentially, she was deciding which children should be sent away and possibly survive and which children should stay with the parents and likely die. In some ways, my mother's fate was worse than ours. She was hard, but no one can be that hard. We lived day to day, making decisions that were forced upon us. My mother was not forced. She was worried about the survival of her family. She looked into the bleak future and knew that making a choice was the smartest thing she could do.

She packed Halina's bag, told her to remove her armband, go onto the road out of town, hitch a ride to the camp, and tell them she was three years older than she was. Halina said her good-byes, walked out to the road crying, and got a ride in a truck to the camp. When she arrived at the camp, she said she had no papers and that she was sixteen. They put her in a prison cell for three days. Then they told her they would accept her in the camp. It was only a few days before the Nazis came to Slomniki to round up the Jews. Laser was shot dead running after my parents from a hiding place. My father was bayonetted. My parents and Sabina were herded into the trucks.

My parents and Sabina were sent to Belzec, where the Nazis murdered them. I did not find out the story until the end of the war. When I did, a stone replaced my heart. I never shed a tear over anything after that, not when Helen died, and not even when my son Joseph died. There was nothing left inside me to trigger the emotion. I would someday feel happiness, joy, love, and elation; but extreme feelings of grief or guilt would be gone forever. I was out of tears. I built a wall. I loved my family. I loved my wife and children, but I would never be able to express it in the way "normal" people would. I would never let anyone get so close that they could bring me to tears. I would cut them out first. The lessons I was learning taught me how to survive, but those skills would not always be helpful when the peace came. Peace never came to me. I struggled with my children, I struggled with my wife, and I struggled with my business ambitions. I struggled for years to stay alive after my doctors told me I would or should be dead. I struggled against my own body. I struggled against my own anger and frustration. I did not want to inherit the wind, but in some ways, I did. Halina told me that she once heard two German guards talking, and one said that even if the Jews survived, they would never know happiness. I did have some happiness, but the closeness and warmth that many others had was lost to me forever.

Not only were the Jews being taken from the villages, the ghettos were also being liquidated. The valuable ones were sent to Plaszow; the others were being sent to extermination camps. Helen was in the ghetto. She was not slated to come to Plaszow. She risked her life as she walked by the guards in the ghetto who were transporting the valuable prisoners to Plaszow. As Helen would have been killed or shipped to an extermination camp when the ghetto was liquidated, she took the risk, hoping they would not check her papers. She walked by the guards, and no one stopped her. She ended up with the ones who were going to Plaszow. When she arrived at the camp, no one bothered to check her papers. She took a big risk, and she was lucky. I guess it ran in the family. Somehow, the three of us were destined to survive. How twisted our reality had become when we had to be thankful for the protection of Amon Göth!

I felt good to have my sisters with me, and I was going to do my best to help them. Göth was making money by renting out Jewish labor to companies in Krakow. I was hired out to a watchmaking shop. Every day I marched into Krakow and went to work in a watchmaker's shop. The owner was a sympathetic Pole, and he was making good money by renting cheap labor. He helped us with extra rations and cigarettes. Some days I came back to the camp with butter, kielbasa, wine, or a large loaf of bread. The camp guards spot-checked the prisoners coming back. Anyone could be searched, and if found with contraband, he or she would be summarily shot. Day after day, I came in with contraband, and I was never stopped. I guess I just had an innocent face. I became so convinced of my destiny that I no longer had any fear. I always shared my extra food with others in the barracks, and I told them the only thing I expected in return was that they should help my sisters if they had a chance. I do not know if it ever paid off, but sharing made me popular, and being popular meant getting favors and information.

I became fluent in German and conversed and traded with the guards. I could have traded with the Ukrainian guards, but I came to detest them. There were many Poles in the camp, but they were either intelligentsia or political activists. They were there for reeducation. I rarely saw the Russian prisoners, but we knew they were getting the worst of it. They were being shot and starved to death every day. Life was actually becoming routine. I knew the rules; I knew when and how to bend them. I came to understand the Germans, their motivations, and how to deal with them. Helen and Halina were being taken care of, and Amon Göth was under investigation by the SS, so he was playing by the rules. For a short time, it seemed as though things were under control.

Halina was chosen for work at Oskar Schindler's factory in Krakow. She marched out with the others in the morning and came back in the evening. In time, Schindler was given permission to build a barracks next to the factory. This made it more efficient for him, as there were no delays in getting the workers to the factory on time. I later learned that he was the only angel in the whole Nazi party, and building the barracks meant the workers were not subject to the brutality of the camp. I was upset at first. I wanted Halina to be near me, and she wanted to stay. At least if there was trouble, I could try to help. I did what I could to get her off Schindler's list. Now she was away, and I had no control over what would happen to her. As it turns out, anyone who knows the story would learn that she was in far better hands.

When Halina came to Plaszow, she had lied about her age in order to get into the camp. At the factory, Schindler made enamelware pots and other cooking utensils for the German Army. Halina would remove the items from the enameling ovens. They were hot and heavy, and she could barely do the job. One day Schindler came walking over and saw her struggling, teetering under the load. When he came up to her, she assumed she was in trouble. She assumed he was as hard and brutal as any other Nazi. He wore that swastika pin on his lapel that was the symbol of all that was horrible in this world. Instead, he offered her a job cleaning his offices. He knew she shouldn't be there.

He was a classic case of a person whose personal morality was far less than shining, but that did not mean he enjoyed the suffering of other people. There were many things I would come to love about America, but I could never understand people's obsession with the personal behavior of our politicians and even presidents. Schindler taught us that there were different aspects of a person's character, and that sex and a little bribery had little or nothing to do with a person making the world a better place.

By the summer of 1944, the Red Army was closing in, and the camp would be liquidated; but first we had to dig up the bodies. The Nazis wanted to get rid of the evidence of their crimes. In particular, they were afraid of the Soviets' desire for revenge at the mass murder of their prisoners. The corpses came apart in our hands. The stench was as unbearable as the physical pain and suffering we had endured. It was made even worse by the huge fires and more stench as the bodies burned around us. If there was a hell, this was truly it.

Halina was shipped off to Auschwitz. I was sure that she would die there. She was given her tattoo, her head was shaved, and she was sent to the showers. Fortunately, it wasn't the gassing showers. She was still too young and healthy. Schindler saved her. It was unheard of. You could be moved to different camps, but if you went into Auschwitz, you did not come out. She did come out and went to Czechoslovakia, where Schindler had a munitions factory, and she lived out the rest of the war. I would not say that Halina had an easy time of it, especially in Auschwitz, but she surely did not suffer as much as she could have. Because of her experience, she retained more of her humanity than the rest of us. She would smile again and perhaps have more joy than we did. To me she was a jewel, a flower that was able to bloom despite the drought. The thought of her surviving gave me that much more determination to go on.

Helen was shipped out to another labor camp. She told me it was much worse than Plaszow. I do not know how she survived, but she did. As the Russians moved west, camps were eradicated, and surviving prisoners were moved west, even into Germany, where the original camps were now more overcrowded than ever. Soon there were no more transports. Prisoners were sent on death marches. Sometimes the guards did not even know where they were headed. The prisoners had no food and almost no water. They just walked. If they fell, they were shot. If they were too slow, they were whipped if they were lucky, or shot if they were not. For many, they could go on no longer and finally gave up. They just fell to the ground and waited to be shot.

Helen was on a march. The war was only a few weeks from ending. She was marching through a German town. The citizens watched, but they no longer jeered or threw stones. They were afraid of what the Allies would do when they found out what happened. Helen had enough. She and a friend left the column and walked into a crowd of civilians. She expected to be shot in the back. She waited for the sound, but the guards did not see her, and not one German from the town opened his or her mouth. The British were fifteen kilometers away. She walked toward them, and in a few days, Helen was finally free. She had made it.

Seven

WANDA: WANDA BRUNER

I believe in one thing only,
the power of human will.

—JOSEF STALIN

I skipped around like an innocent young girl in front of the guards, a piece of paper in my hand, swinging it around. Sometimes I would drop it and pick it up. They smiled. The world had turned ugly, but I knew they would smile at the innocence of a girl, skipping around on the street, not a thought in her head. It was a moment's respite for the soldiers. This world was on fire. No quarter was given. Russian prisoners would be exterminated just as German prisoners would, and all civilians were fair game for the armies. I was just a butterfly, a fleeting moment of peace and remembrance that there were some good memories from before the war.

Now was when I needed my courage. Now was the time to use the wits the soldiers did not think I had. It was time to size them up based on the looks on their faces. It was time to be quick—as quick as I was at grabbing a pigeon when it just started to take off from the ground; as quick as when I chased a jackrabbit down an alley, cornered it, and grabbed it by the neck. I needed to be as sneaky as when I slipped into the backyards of peasants who raised rabbits and chickens and took them without being caught. My father's life depended on my skill, and I would do anything not to let him down.

I did not always have the skills I had now. I was never in need of real survival skills. Not in Jaroslav, Poland, before the war. I was happy. My father was a tailor, and my mother worked in a bakery. Their names were Rachael and Marcus Drapacz (pronounced drah-pahtch). My relatives pronounced it "draypez" after coming to America. Somehow, it sounded more French and sophisticated instead of the earthy, peasant Slavic name that it was. My father was tall and walked with long strides. My mother was short, not quite five feet. One foot was shorter than the other. She walked on the ball of her foot on her short leg. You always knew when she was coming because the heel of her shoe would be dragging. We made our own clothes, we baked our bread, and I went to the public school and sat at Mass every morning. We were poor, but I had my share of fun. Though Jaroslav was a city, we did not live in a Jewish area. We lived in a house with a vegetable garden. We got along with our neighbors. We wished one another well during our respective holidays.

Every Saturday morning, my father would walk to shul where he would spend the day discussing Torah and current events with the other Jewish men of the village. The women would bring a large fish so the men could continue all day. I was the oldest of four children. Once a week, a very funny-looking man called Tooley came to the village with his goat. My mother gave me some money. I gave it to Tooley, and he would milk his goat directly into a large tin mug. Many children stood in line for Tooley's milk. If my mother found out I used the money for something else, I would be in a lot of trouble. She considered it essential for my health.

I would play games in the town square with my friends. I would always look up at the balcony of a restaurant where the upper-class Poles ate, drank, and looked down on the peasants. There were women in beautiful dresses, men in fine dark suits, and the dashing Polish cavalry officers in their white uniforms. It would be forty years before I would come with Mates, sit on that balcony, and look down on the Poles. It would take a long time, but it would be satisfying.

My family was all around, and I felt loved and protected. I had a younger sister and two younger brothers. My grandmother spent a lot of time with me. She fawned over me and made me feel so special. That she died in the war was my greatest loss, and I never forgot her. I had cousins, aunts, and uncles who always came over. My favorite was my uncle David, my mother's brother. When he was young, he lived in this area under czarist Russia. The czar's elite guard was made up of the Cossacks[8] from the Ukraine, who were also notorious anti-Semites. My uncle was not your stereotypical Jew. He was tall and strong, with massive shoulders. He was blond haired and blue eyed, and he was fearless. The Cossacks came riding through his village on their beautiful horses with royal-looking uniforms and their long, curved sabers. They were looking for recruits. They saw Uncle David on the street and offered him the honor. He told them he was a Jew. They told him he was no Jew, only a coward. They beat him, tied him up, and took him away. As far as we knew, Uncle David was the only Jewish Cossack.

He lived an exciting life, and I loved his stories and could listen for hours when he came to visit, riding in on his horse in an immaculate uniform. He would put his sword in the closet. I was told never to touch it. One day, I sneaked into the closet and pulled out the shining saber. Surely he must have slashed a few of the czar's enemies with it. It was unfair to be a girl. I wanted to be a Cossack like Uncle David. I wanted to be a Polish cavalry officer in a white uniform with braids hanging from my shoulders. I liked to march around and pretend I was a soldier. I ran my hand over the razor-sharp blade and cut my palm. I could hardly feel it at first. Then the blood started flowing, and I screamed. After my mother bandaged my hand, she gave me a slap across the face. A Cossack's sword was not to be unsheathed unless it was going to be used. Uncle David was not mad. He thought I had spunk.

---

8 See "Chmelnitsky" in the Appendix.

From Hell's Heart

When Poland became independent, Uncle David became an officer in the Polish cavalry, but we still called him a Cossack. By the time the war came, he was old and retired. My father and he used to talk politics. While they were in agreement with each other, they were at odds with their peers. My father had worked in Germany after the First World War. He listened to the radio, and he believed it was far more ominous than mere rhetoric. He said the Nazis meant every word, and they would invade. He did not like the Germans. Though Germany was weak because of the Treaty of Versailles, he knew they would rebuild, and so did Uncle David. It was a simple equation to my father. To the west was a militaristic, totalitarian dictatorship. To the east, there was a militaristic totalitarian dictatorship. In the middle was Poland. Wasn't it obvious where the battleground would be? It did not really matter. There was nowhere to go. There was no money for us to travel, and there were no visas to be had.

It was easier to pretend that this would blow over. The Jews had faced persecution in the past. Times would be tough. Some would die. We would work and suffer; and in time, it would pass. This was the cycle since the Jews came to this area so long ago. Nothing could have been worse than what the Ukrainians did in the Chmelnitsky[9] uprising where our hands were cut off, our abdomens opened, and cats sewn inside. That was a long time ago, and surely the world was more civilized...or so the other Jews believed. There were pogroms in Jaroslav after World War I. They happened off and on from 1918 until 1921. People died, property was lost, but eventually things got better. This is how it was for the Jews of Europe. We were poor. It took a lifetime to afford a house. It took almost as long to buy a piece of good furniture. To leave was unthinkable. Besides, who could stand against those dashing, beautiful Polish cavalry officers?

The war did come. Maybe I was stupid, but it was the most excitement I had ever had. People hid in their houses from the Stuka dive bombers. They had a siren on the front that was meant to terrorize the

9 See Appendix.

people. I stayed outside and watched the bombs go off and listened to the screams of the Stukas' sirens. My mother came outside and grabbed me by the hair to drag me inside. I didn't see what the problem was. After all, the Poles were going to win, and war was thrilling compared to our hard daily lives.

Within two weeks, the Germans came driving into town. Everyone was issued papers. The Orthodox had to shave their beards, or the Germans would do it for them. My father was more modern, so he did not have a beard to shave. We didn't particularly stand out as Jewish, so there was no immediate harassment. The Russians invaded from the east. The border was the San River on the east side of town. Many talked about going over to the Russians if things got worse. Uncle David ignored the Germans and went about his business. One day a German officer stopped him and asked for his papers. Uncle David spewed out a few choice Polish obscenities, spat on the ground, and walked away. The officer drew his pistol and put an end to Uncle David. At least he died with dignity. I am sure he would rather have been dead than live through the nightmare that was coming.

The Germans banged on our doors with their rifles. We all came outside. The Jews had one hour to gather what they could carry and march across the bridge to the Russian zone. We went inside to pack. My mother did not want to leave. "Marcus, we'll be better off here. We have family nearby. We can sneak out the back and run."

As always, my father was cool, reasonable, and gentle. "Rachael, there is nothing for us here. If we are caught, we will all be shot. Even if we could stay, I know what the Germans will do to us. I listen to the German broadcasts. I read the Yiddish papers. I know what they are already doing in Germany. Believe me, this is a blessing."

The Germans liked order. The Jews had to be processed. There were too many Jews to process in an orderly fashion. They had captured Poland faster than they had thought. The population had to be fed. Refugees were everywhere. The more Jews they could push from Eastern Poland over to the Russians, the better. It was less paperwork.

From Hell's Heart

We marched before the German soldiers. When we came to the bridge over the river San, everyone was pushing and shoving. The Germans were pushing from behind and shooting anyone who straggled. There was yelling, screaming, crying.

This war was no longer something for me to observe. It was time to suffer. I just hoped they did not kill my father. They were quick to kill the men, but he spoke German and followed their commands. My mother wanted to resist. My father told her simply that these were Germans. An order had been given, and to the Germans, any order was to be followed. The crowd on the bridge was too much. People fell over the side and drowned. It was chaos, but we would soon be safe on the Russian side. When the last of the Jews got on the bridge, the Germans blew it up, killing many families. We were already on the other side because my father made my mother hurry up and not pack too much.

The Russians put us in barracks. We unpacked the few belongings we brought. My father tried to find work, and I learned Russian as fast as I could. It wasn't hard at my age. The Russians were not like the Germans. They were not cruel for cruelty's sake. They had some pity, and they could be kind to a young girl like me. They did have strict rules. Violating them would mean long prison terms, or you could be summarily shot. My mother missed her family that was still in the German zone. Some people were going back to bring supplies to their families. We heard it was very bad on the German side, and there were even fewer rations for the Jews than the Poles. They had no coffee, no sugar, and no flour. They were lucky if they had enough potatoes, flour, and butter to last a week. Life was becoming hard, and I was slowly becoming harder inside. I was less moved by the misery of others, because I was more concerned with the well-being of my immediate family.

My mother, less than five feet tall, with a crippled leg and babushka on her head, went to a Russian officer to bribe him so she could get on a truck and get over to the German zone. They were allies, after all. She saw the trucks go back and forth every day. The searches were cursory. Others were doing it.

We were now under the reign of Marshal Stalin. We were subject to his whims, his paranoia, and his desire to eliminate threats that could occur in the future. Whether there was any possibility of a threat was irrelevant; Stalin did not need reasons—a fantasy was enough. He moved whole populations out of their homelands and resettled the areas with people who had moved from their homelands, just in case the people had a desire for a nationalist uprising. He saw spies everywhere. Now that there was war, he knew, as Hitler did, that it was only a matter of time before they were no longer allies. That meant that anyone could be a German spy, especially those who had come from the German zone. If the Germans hated Jews, then how did these Jews escape? Why would a Jew want to go back to the German zone if she was endangered by doing so? My father warned my mother that her plan was endangering the family.

The Russians now banged on our door with their rifles. When we came outside, we were told we had one hour to pack what we could carry. We, and many other Jews from the area of Jaroslav, were packed into a train car with food, water, a stove, and toilet buckets. The door was shut and locked from the outside. At the time, it seemed like a tremendous hardship. My father was furious with my mother and blamed her plan to sneak over to the German Zone for our misfortune. It turns out this was another blessing. The Germans would overrun the rest of Poland in 1941 and drive deep into Russia, but we were too far east. Whatever hardship we were to face, we would survive by our wits and our resourcefulness. For all those Jews under German rule, only a few would have this luxury. Death was all too arbitrary for too many millions to even ponder. Stalin once said that the death of a few hundred or a few thousand people was a tragedy—the death of millions was just a statistic.

The train stopped, the soldiers opened the door, and we got out. We were at the train station in Kazan, where we stayed for about two weeks. We were put on a train again and stopped about five kilometers outside of Yoshkar-Ola. There was an open field surrounded by forest, and everything was covered with snow. We were in the foothills of the Urals, and now we would learn what it was truly like to be cold. We helped the soldiers unload the train cars. They helped us build Quonset hut barracks. Then the soldiers left. There were about twenty families in the building. We were on our own, and we weren't in Poland anymore.

My son Joe once asked me why we didn't hunt in the forest. I told him, "What Jew knew how to hunt? We were city people. We bought our food in the market, and we picked berries and mushrooms in the fields. We knew nothing of guns and hunting." Every day I walked deep into the dark forest, at least five kilometers. I picked berries and mushrooms. My mother had taught me what to pick. I would like to say that she learned it from her mother, but she was an orphan. She worked for another family, just as an orphan had worked for Mates's family. One day she was walking in a field and fell into a sinkhole. She broke her leg. She had no money for a doctor and no family to take care of her. She wrapped her leg in a splint, rested for a week, and went back to work. The leg stopped growing.

When I had a sled full of baskets filled with berries and mushrooms, I would walk out of the forest and another five kilometers to the village and sell them in the market. Then I would come home. I walked at least ten to fifteen kilometers a day. Sometimes I would get very tired. The snow looked so inviting. It would be easy to rest awhile in the soft snow, but everyone in Russia knew the consequences of falling asleep in the snow. I learned at such a young age what hard work was. Even worse was going to the forest to chop wood and drag it back on the sled. I was only thirteen. I felt like a farm animal, but there was no choice. You had to survive. There was no work for my parents. We learned to hustle. My father wasn't very good at it. He did sewing as he could get work. My mother had learned to hustle as an orphan. She was a good teacher for me. Once a week, a man would come to our hut with goat carcasses all skinned and gutted. You could say he was a traveling butcher. My mother and the other women would crowd around him to distract him. I was shorter, and he could not see me below the women. Out came my knife, and I would slice off a nice piece of goat and run away.

Pretty soon I learned to catch pigeons and rabbits. I did not catch rats. I do not know if I would have eaten a cat or a dog. I would like to think that I would not, but it did not matter. I never saw one where I was. They had already been eaten. I don't know if there were any cats or dogs left in Russia. I loved animals. I liked furry, cute rabbits. We never ate them before because they were not kosher. I had a dog when I was little. He was run over by a car, and we always had cats around the house to catch mice and rats. I did not want to eat those animals that I kept as pets. You have to understand what it was like to be hungry. You have to be starving. I saw the civilians who were evacuated from Leningrad. They were bones with eyes sticking out. You could not tell a man from a woman. There were no animals left in Leningrad, not even mice or rats. They were missing a few orphan children also. They started disappearing after all the animals were gone. Hunger will make you mad, and cannibalism was not unheard of during the war. I considered myself lucky. I did not have to eat rats, but I did learn that a rabbit or pigeon could do nicely if you were hungry enough. You know, you have to be able to close one eye sometimes, or you just won't make it.

We were now truly strangers in a strange land. This land once belonged to the Tatars, Turks of the Golden Horde from the east who had once ruled Russia. They were olive skinned, some turbaned, good with horses, and Muslim. Just as many were Christian, as the czars had forced them to convert. The churches, mosques, and synagogues were open again. Stalin would use any means to keep up the people's spirits. If propaganda and threats were not enough, they could look to God if they wanted to. Besides, the Americans were sending a lot of aid, and all they asked for was a little religious freedom.

I learned to deal in the black market: vodka, flour, tobacco, shoes, boots, and sugar. I cut the sugar with flour. I cut the flour with talc. It was the only way to make a profit. It was illegal and could be punishable by summary execution. I was of great value to the adults. Much of our activity took place at or near the grand bazaar. The streets were narrow and crowded. When the police chased an adult, he or she would hand me the backpack, and I would run through the market. I was too small to be seen. All the adults towered over me. I could not be followed. I was a swift runner. I was a reliable courier. Who would think to stop a girl?

Here I was, skipping around in the snow, just waiting for the right moment to slip past these guards. I wore my nicest clothes, too, so I would look cute for all the adults I had to fool that day. It was a khaki-green yarn outfit with leggings, skirt, blouse, cap, and mittens. The women of America sat in their homes, knitting watch caps, socks, sweaters, and gloves for the boys fighting the war. The Americans also sent aid. It was the first time I knew anything about Americans. We had flour and grain sacks with an American flag on them. I could not read the words, and the government wanted us to think they were providing it, but no one was fooled. We even learned an American word for a car. It was called a jeep. The government said they were made in a secret factory deep in the Urals, but if you looked at one closely, you could see the letters "USA." How could these people be fighting the Germans and the Japanese and still send us food, cars, and trucks?

They also sent us useless gloves. Didn't they know that we needed mittens, or our fingers would freeze? Didn't they know that you needed more than a watch cap? Socks? Who needed socks? You wrapped your feet in layers of wool and put them in soft, felt-lined boots. Hard, shiny leather boots would freeze and crack. We tanned the leather until it was soft and supple. It did not hold a shine, but it would not crack. The sweaters were OK, but we liked the kind with buttons on the front. We wore them in layers and could open them up when we started sweating. You didn't even need buttons. You just wrapped a belt around you.

This stuff was good enough for the spring and fall, but it was useless in the winter. Instead, I pulled everything apart—all those watch caps, gloves, and socks—and knitted myself a nice outfit. I wasn't crazy about the color, but I had to close one eye. The Americans probably did not know just how cold it got in Russia, but I heard the Germans were downright stupid. They wore helmets and wool coats with scarves, shiny leather boots, and gloves. It was no wonder they were losing the war.

The best thing the Americans made was great movies. I will never forget *Casablanca*. It was released in Russia as part of the wartime propaganda effort. It was the first romantic movie I saw in my life. Ingrid Bergman was the prettiest woman I ever saw, and Humphrey Bogart was the bravest man next to my uncle David. The theme song became my theme song. I hummed it when I worked. I sang it when I trudged through the deep snow so I would not fall asleep. I sang it to my babies.

The time had come; the soldiers were bored and had lost interest in watching me. I bolted between them, running as fast as I could. As I shot by them, I saw the door that said "Commissar." Another second, and I would be at the door, but the guards grabbed me. I screamed, I scratched, and I made it sound like I was being slaughtered alive. Before they could drag me out, the door flew open. A true Russian stepped out. He was blond, tall, and big-shouldered. His pants were stuffed into his boots, his fists were on his hips, and he wore the silly looking, oversized epaulets that the Russians started using when they joined the Allies. "What is going on here? What is this little girl doing here? Is she your prisoner, or did she get by you?"

"We are sorry, Comrade Commissar. She ran between us. We will get rid of her."

"No, you cannot," I screamed. "My father will die if you don't sign this prescription."

"What are you talking about, little girl?" he asked.

It was time to talk fast. "My father has pneumonia and is in the hospital, dying. He was at home, and my mother sat next to him saying prayers, waiting for him to die. I told her we have to get him to the hospital. She said there was no help for civilians at the hospital, only soldiers and party members. I told her we had to try. We wrapped him in blankets and put him on my sled. I dragged him ten kilometers to the hospital. The doctor said he did not have the sulfa drugs to help him. The doctor gave me a prescription. I ran another five kilometers to the pharmacy, but the pharmacist said the prescription was no good unless you signed it, or she could be shot. You have to sign it. You cannot let my father die."

The commissar took the prescription from my hand. He filled in the quantity and signed it. I ran back to the pharmacy. They gave me a huge quantity of sulfa packets. I said I did not need that much, but she had no choice because that was the quantity on the form. I ran back to the hospital and gave the drugs to the doctor. I came to the hospital every day to make sure my father got his medication. He walked out of that hospital. The doctor wanted to know what he should do with the rest of the sulfa drugs. I told him to keep them. Years later when I told this story to Mates, he said the doctor would only sell it to patients who could pay. I did not care. My father was alive, and that was all that mattered. Dealing in vodka was one thing. Trading in medicine was another.

I never knew exactly why the commissar helped me. Death was not a shocking event to the Russians. Most people had already experienced the First World War, the revolution, the civil war, the secret police, the gulags, Stalin's purges, the mass killings, Stalin's forced famine in the Ukraine, and now this war. Millions more would die before it was over. The Russian people knew nothing about peace. I suspect this man realized his power to help one little girl and used it. Perhaps I reminded him of something good or why they were fighting this war. I do know that in the midst of horror and destruction, I saw, at times, great acts of kindness and courage. The Russians could be brutal, but with a little vodka, they could just as easily be your best friends.

Later, my father was taken into the army. He was too old to fight, but they needed tailors. He went to the local synagogue and asked if he could have a tallit so he could say his prayers while he was away. They were old and ragged around the neck, probably from before the revolution, but they gave him one. It had no prayer around the collar, no fancy needlework. It was as plain and simple as we were. We went to the train station to see him off.

Hundreds of families were there every day, crying as their young sons went off to a war that seemed like nothing more than a monster consuming young men by the millions. Once the Germans made war on the

Russians, they both lost a lot of men. Russian tanks and planes were not as good as the German equipment, but the Russians had one thing the Germans would never have. They had an inexhaustible supply of people. Five hundred thousand men were drafted every single month for the duration of the war. They froze, and they were hungry. Many did not have rifles. They had to wait for the man in front to be shot so they could pick up his. They were used to march across minefields because trucks and tanks were far too valuable. They could not run away because the commissars would have them shot. They could not afford to be captured. Either the Germans would send them to concentration camps, or Stalin would think they were spies if they escaped or were liberated. To be a Jew and a Russian soldier made it worse, if there could be such a thing. To be captured meant death. The Russians and partisans pushed them into the front lines. They did not have names. They were all referred to as Abramchik.

We did not expect to see my father again, but there were so many miracles during the war. He found us. We finished the war as an intact family.

For the rest of the war, I continued my illicit activities. I was sharp and bold. Every day I went to work at the kolkhoz (communal farm). After digging my quota of potatoes from the hard, frozen soil, I was allowed to go and pick potatoes for myself. I had made a mark on the ground where I found the small, round potatoes. I covered them up and went back at the end of the day. You could fit a lot more potatoes into a bucket because the small potatoes fit together better and did not waste space. I wasn't going to school, but I figured out a little geometry. The same was true of melons and cabbages.

The rabbits were not kosher, and my mother would not eat them, but she allowed us to. Religion had to be set aside for the sake of the children. One day we spooned some of the juice onto my mother's potatoes and cabbage because we wanted her to be healthy. She could taste it right away and refused to eat it. Horseflesh is also not kosher, but we could eat it if we could get it. I came upon a dead horse too late. It had already been cut up, but the head was intact. I brought the head home and put it in a big pot to boil all day. When I took it out, it was still very tough, so I put it back in and let it boil until the next day. I would take out the head and chew on the meaty parts and put it back in the pot. I chewed on the head for a few days. Ask anyone who went through the war, and they will tell you the same thing: of all the different ways to suffer, hunger is the worst. It will drive people mad, and before long, they will do anything for food.

Somehow, we survived the war. For some reason I always had an attachment to Russia and its people. It was dark, mysterious, but full of life. Everyone was a comrade. Instead of the wealthy aristocrats looking down on the peasants, the peasants were now in charge. You were not looked down upon because your speech was colloquial. Stalin himself had come from Georgia. Stalin did some horrible things, but his actions saved my family. My grandson, Jesse, likes history and politics. I told him, if anyone starts bad-mouthing Stalin, you should spit on him. Were it not for Stalin, Jesse would not exist.

When the war was over, we went back to Poland—my mother, my father, my sister Elsa, and my brothers, Abram and Gerry. Gerry was only about eleven years old when the war ended. For such a young child to survive was a tribute to the rest of us. We did not return to Jaroslav. Some of the Poles we met along the way were surprised to see a whole family of Jews. They thought all the Jews had died, and here was an entire family of six. Not only had we survived, but we looked healthier than the Poles.

A Polish woman was talking to my mother. She asked her if we had been to a resort for the last six years. We had heard the stories of Jews who had come back to reclaim their possessions and were killed. My father had more sense than that. We headed for Waldenburg. There was a large Zionist organization there that was helping to gather refugees together and smuggle them into Palestine or wait there until the British lifted the embargo. We'd had enough of Europe, and Europe had had enough of us, especially the Poles. There was a saying that the Germans did not put so many camps in Poland for nothing. Between the Poles and the Ukrainians, they knew they would have eager helpers. Many Poles blamed the Jews for the war. For all the Poles had suffered, the mentality of many did not change. The Jews' fate, some believed, was God's punishment, but the Nazis did not need God's help for the destruction they had brought on Europe. They did just fine on their own. I do know one thing: as much as I was jealous over not being born a man, if the world were run by women, there would not have been a war. I also came to believe that the world would be better off if there were not so many religions.

Eight

AUNT BERTA: SAM BRUNER

It was a funeral that nobody wanted. Not that anybody ever wants a funeral, but some are worse than others. When I heard that Berta had cancer and was not expected to live, I said to my mother, "This is going to hurt a lot." My mother agreed completely. The few family deaths we suffered hurt, of course, but this would hurt just a little more. So far, Jacob and Helen had passed, and I missed them both. We simply were not used to death. Anyone who had any genetic weakness died during the war. The war was a filter. There were not many left from that generation, but the ones who survived were an awfully tough bunch of Polacks.

I was OK at the beginning of the funeral. Everyone was solemn. The rabbi had been well prepped by my cousins for the eulogy. When he started talking about Berta's kitchen, the tears just started flowing from my eyes, and I could not stop. I had brought no tissues, because I did not expect to cry. I had not cried at a funeral yet. I was just sad, but the mention of Berta's kitchen was too much. It was a symbol, just as it was for my mother. Something was always cooking in there: pierogi, kreplach, *palushskis*, latkes, kugel, and strudel. Deb had brought tissues. She was always prepared. As long as Deb knew me, I had spoken little about Berta and rarely taken Deb to visit her. Why, she wondered, was I suddenly so upset? It was the connection to my childhood. The rabbi mentioned the kitchen, and I was transported back in an instant. It was a childhood of mixed feelings and emotions, but the mention of Berta brought thoughts of kindness, gentleness, and warmth.

Berta was my father's half sister. She and Daneck lived in Philadelphia, and we visited them often when we were young. These were the *greenas* (Yiddish for green). Once you understood that, a lot of the strangeness fell in place. Part of the greena mentality was to visit family to the exclusion of any social circle. There was no social circle, just family. Many Saturday nights, we went to Berta and Daneck's. It got boring. The family talked about the same things, not that we could understand much as they were speaking Polish. We watched TV, we did homework, and we got bored eventually. If there was a consolation, it was food.

As I sat at the funeral, a scene came into my mind. It was walking into Berta's house. Out she came from the kitchen. She was tall and heavy. The few words of Yiddish that we learned included "zaftig," and Berta was the example. "Samela," she said in a squeaky, high-pitched, heavy accent. Neither she nor Daneck could speak much English, and what they could say was barely understandable. She would dance over and give me a big, wet kiss. She would lean down, hug me, squeeze me into her ample bosom, and then slip me a freshly made pierogi.

She fed me chicken soup with kreplach, and she made the best strudel in the world with apples, strawberries, nuts, and raisins. One small piece weighed so much and gave me heartburn, but it was so worth it. In my mind, Berta vied with my mother as the best cook in the family. The main difference was that my mother had heard about cholesterol, so at some point she used butter to cook with instead of chicken fat. Mom would let the soup cool in the "Frigidaire." (All refrigerators were Frigidaires. Bess Myerson, the first Jewish Miss America, sold them, so they had to be good.) When the soup was cool, she would scrape the fat off the top. Berta never let modern science get in the way of her cooking. Schmaltz was the stuff of life. You spread it on rye bread instead of butter. It was all salt and fat, and it made everything taste better. She could no more stop cooking with schmaltz than some Southerners could stop using Crisco. The best treat was chicken rinds and chicken livers fried in chicken fat. In her living room was a candy dish that was always full of M&Ms.

Unfortunately, along with Berta came Daneck. When Daneck greeted you, he grabbed your cheek and pinched it really hard. Then he grabbed your hand to shake it, and he squeezed your hand really hard and moved the knuckle that attached your hand to your pinkie back and forth. Daneck thought that was tremendously funny. I am sure he thought it was an endearing quality. I had to wait a lot of years until I was strong enough to do the same to him. It was possibly as satisfying as when my mother sat on the balcony of the restaurant in her hometown.

Daneck was a war hero. He was short, squat, and strong. He was called up into the Polish army before my father. He was already married to Berta, so they lived in Boryslaw. That meant he was in the Russian zone, and when Germany invaded Russia, he became part of the Polish brigade serving with the Red Army under the Russians.

Daneck got along well with the Russians. He was a peasant at heart. He didn't read books, and he didn't discuss ideas. He was boorish and crude. He liked big women, vodka, and dirty jokes, and he cursed a lot. This was no counterrevolutionary. He became a noncommissioned officer in the tank corps. He was not educated enough or of a high enough rank for Stalin to murder as Poland neared liberation. He chose the tank corps for a few good reasons: the tank protected him from bullets, he would not have to march in the snow, and it was heated.

Daneck was in a number of major battles. The Battle of Kursk was the worst battle of the war. Kursk was either the largest or one of the largest armored battles in history. Over two million men would fight in this one battle, and no quarter would be given. Those who surrendered would be shot or taken away as slave laborers. Only a trickle would ever see home again. If either side retreated without orders, either the SS or the commissars would shoot them.

The tank battles were horrific. Nothing could stand against the newest German tanks. A German tank could shoot a Russian tank long before the German tank was in range of the Russian tank. The Allies in the West had the same problem. The question was numbers. While the Germans produced thousands of tanks in a year, the Allies produced tens of thousands. The only strategy was to surround the German tank, get close, and hit it on the side where the armor was weakest.

The Battle of Kursk would be like Armageddon, and Daneck was in the middle of it. He was under the main hatch, loading shells, when his tank was hit. He popped out of the open hatch while the other men burned to death. When he hit the ground, he was on fire and rolled around to put it out. He took a bullet near his stomach. This was a small-time wound in that army. He was patched up and put back into a new tank. The Polish brigade liberated Lvov and, of course, Boryslaw. Daneck was a returning hero to his countrymen, and he went looking for Berta.

I grew up seeing a happy, kind, cheerful woman with a great heart. As I got older, I learned how much heartache a person could have without being in a concentration camp. I also had no idea that men coveted her for more than her pierogis.

My grandfather Herschel was married in Boryslaw, and his wife gave birth to Berta, David, Mundick, and Simon. Berta's mother died when she was a child. Eventually, as Berta entered her young teens, Herschel met Golda and decided to get married again. Berta did not get along with her new stepmother; in fact, the whole family was against the marriage. Herschel saw no solution, so he left what money and possessions he had and moved to Krakow with Golda. The maternal grandparents raised Berta and her brothers in Boryslaw. Herschel and Golda had five children, all born in Krakow. There were trips back and forth. The children seemed to hold no grudges against one another, and when the war came, they helped one another.

Just before the SS came to Boryslaw, the Nazis allowed Ukrainian nationalists and Polish sympathizers who allied themselves with the Nazis to stage a pogrom lasting three days. Berta and her brothers tried to hide. The youngest, Simon, was found. During the three-day orgy of violence, Jewish men, women, and children were cut to pieces, beaten, and shot. At the end of the three days, Berta, David, and Mundick came out into the streets where the mutilated corpses lay. Hands, feet, and women's breasts were nailed to walls. They found Simon with part of his head caved in. They took him to the cemetery at night, buried him, and then went into hiding again.

A few days after the pogrom, the SS came through the area, shooting and creating their own new mass graves. They started processing the Jews and other undesirables and handing out the armbands. David had a family, I am told. They died during the war. My father said David never spoke about it when he asked. David and Mundick went through the war and somehow survived.

Berta had her own story. Daneck was off fighting the war. Berta did not know what would happen to her or whether she would ever see Daneck again. There was an older man in Boryslaw who liked Berta very much. He had built a bunker in the woods and had made himself comfortable, at least relative to a concentration camp. He offered to let Berta come and live with him. Berta took him up on the offer. No one knew whether or not she loved him or, if she did, if she loved him more than Daneck. To me, there seems little doubt that the mutual fear and the protection they provided each other had to create a bond. It would be three years before she would see Daneck again. A lot can happen in a bunker over three years.

A number of people hid in the woods like this. In some ways, it could be worse than a labor camp. In a camp, if you lived by the rules and did not get sick, there was a chance you could survive. Most importantly, you were not being hunted. You did not live with the uncertainty that at any moment German soldiers, the SS, or even partisans would hunt you down and kill you the moment they saw you. You could not show your face to anyone. Food was scarce, and the winters were harsh. When the rain came, you lived in mud.

This is how Berta survived, but her troubles were not over just because the war ended. She stayed in the woods. She came into town to find out if Daneck had come back. Daneck had come back. He was a hero, and he had a rifle. There was no law. There were only conquering heroes. The family kept quiet for a time. Finally they told Daneck where he could find Berta. He took his rifle and went to the bunker in the woods. Only Berta was there. She did not know what to do. She knew she was his wife, and she was afraid Daneck would kill her lover. Daneck looked around and saw some nice furniture and a sewing machine. He started to pack things up. Berta became frantic as the chance of the two men meeting grew greater. She begged Daneck to leave. She told him she would come with him and stay with him forever if he would only leave now. He agreed, and they moved into an apartment.

Berta's lover came to town looking for her. He was soon apprised of a few simple facts. Daneck was Berta's legal husband. Berta went back to him of her own free will and to spare him from Daneck's anger. If Daneck wanted to kill him, he could. No one could stop him, and there would be no retribution. The lover walked out of Berta's life forever. Whether Berta truly loved him and wanted to be with him instead of Daneck, no one would ever know. All I knew was that this cheery, hefty, happy woman had been in a lover's triangle in her youth in the midst of war.

Berta desperately wanted a child, but life was cheating her again. She knew of a young Polish woman who was pregnant and did not want the baby. Berta and Daneck took the baby soon after it was born. She named him Simon after her brother, and she was very happy. In time, they noticed that Simon was a little slow in developing. He was mentally disabled, and he got worse with time. David, Mundick, Berta, and Daneck moved to Israel after independence. Berta and Daneck came to the United States about 1959. I was quite young. They stayed in our small, rented row house until they found work and settled in the Philadelphia area. Simon fell farther and farther behind other children. By the time he was sixteen, he was uncontrollable. If he did not get what he wanted, he would hit Berta and Daneck. He had grown quite tall. One day, he pulled a knife on Daneck. They sent him to an institution and brought him home on weekends. Berta and Daneck could only watch as their nieces and nephews grew, went to college, got married, and had children. Berta never showed her disappointment with life. The only time I saw her cry was in the hospital as she was dying.

Nine

ALIENATION

I will never understand some of the things my father did regarding his choice of where to raise his children, though he claims he had his reasons. Some of it seemed out of ignorance at best, and at worst, it came from a simple lack of forethought or indifference to his children. He created a world that alienated him, his wife, and his children from the community around him. It would take a good part of my adult life before I could understand that he was so antisocial that the alienation created something of a cocoon for him, holding back a world that could become hostile again at any time. He could show the world his public face and retreat into his private world, where he could be himself.

"Dad," I asked one day, "if you don't believe in God, then why do you insist I go to Hebrew school?" This was a complicated subject. Some parents dropped their children at the front door and never came in. That was my experience.

"What I believe is not important," he told me. "There is more to Judaism than belief in God. My parents died because they were Jewish, and I do this out of respect for them. You will eventually make your own decisions, but at least I did my duty." Wow! That was surely a ringing endorsement of the importance of going to Hebrew school twice a week, services on Saturday, Sunday school, and the extra homework during the week. That pretty well cut out after-school sports until after my bar mitzvah.

If you do not understand what a Jewish education is, it involves learning Hebrew, learning about the Bible, and Jewish history. You weren't just talking about the Bible and faith. There is a saying in the Talmud that an ignorant person can never be truly pious. That is not exactly Christian dogma. Knowing Joe's personality and his need for a good reason for doing something, it was no wonder he refused to do work that was totally irrelevant to him. Going to services was the worst experience. The service was almost all in Hebrew and went on for a minimum of two and a half hours. To so many of us it was just mumbling, going through the motions, repeating the same prayers over and over until they had no meaning. It was just what you were supposed to do. You had a duty, an obligation, and that is a far cry from faith. The only thing that had meaning to me was the music. It was a beautiful connection. The tunes were mostly in the minor mode and gave the melodies a very haunting, almost painful quality that seemed to echo ages of faith and emotion.

When I was a Scout, on Sundays while on camping trips, the troops put on their dress uniforms and were divided by religious groupings and taken to church. They did not want to leave me alone at the campsite, so I had to choose where to go. I chose whichever church did not have a huge crucifix with a man hanging from it covered in gashes and blood. That this was God made little or no sense to me any more than the Trinity does today. It was clear that these people relied more on faith than tradition, and their faith was not based on a duty, but on the desire for salvation.

As to alienation, I always wondered why my father decided to live in communities with so few Jewish families. He always said that he wanted to show others that he was no different. He wanted to be an example because of his experiences. I think this was noble in and of itself, but it did not take into account his children. It meant not having Jewish friends and, when the time came, no selection of Jewish girls to go out with.

The synagogue we belonged to was located in a different community, and those children were in a different school district. Aside from seeing them at the synagogue, there was no other interaction. The community we lived in was part of a large school district to which our community was not connected. That meant long bus rides and no after-school interaction with the majority of children who attended those schools. My junior high-school years were particularly tough. Out of about twelve hundred students, I was aware of only three or four Jewish kids. Anyone knows that seventh- and eighth-grade children can be particularly hard on one another.

I could feel the force of the kick or the push as my books went flying out from under my arms followed either by "Hey, Jew boy," or "Hey, Jew nose." I had to keep calm and first see if there was more than one wise guy, and even if there was only one, how big he was. If it looked like a fair fight, it would have to happen after school. If they were much bigger than me, then I had to learn to swallow my pride, though I must say, I lost it one day and went after someone bigger than me. He was winning, but he was suffering enough that it would no longer be worth his trouble. We were stopped by a teacher and suspended for a week. His family was no happier than mine with his getting suspended for fighting, so we pretty much steered clear of each other after that.

My father was very upset with me. I was not supposed to fight back. Why, then, was I put into this school? My mother understood, yet my father thought there was some kind of lesson in being pushed around and controlling your temper. Now that I am much older, I can see the value in it, but I would never put my kids through it.

Even in high school with the "neighborhood gang," I had to get used to Jewish jokes or be without some local friends. I don't hold a grudge. Kids will latch onto whatever makes someone different. Most of them were Italian or Irish, so they did not make jokes about themselves. Had I been a member of any minority, they would have used it against me. What bothered me later, after I went to college, was thinking back about how some of my friends, though never making Jewish jokes at my expense, still were loath to stand up for me. Once I started college, I let most of those friendships drop. I was lucky in some respects. I had two friends whom I could count on and whose families always made me feel welcome. These weren't just friends I hung out with; these were homes I went to so I could be out of my house with all the arguing and my parents talking about divorce. As far as Bob, Sue, and their parents, I was lucky to feel so welcome at the homes of an Irish family and an Italian family.

My father never did "get it" when it came to these issues. My mother did. She listened, and she understood, but she did not rule the roost. All the relatives on both sides of the family warned my father about not raising his children in Jewish neighborhoods. Looking back, they were right. My father had his own ideas, and there was little anyone could do to change his mind.

"Look at this picture," my aunt Elsa said, raising her voice. It was a photo my mother found in the attic of a group picture from scout camp. "Except for Sammy, there is not one other Jew. Not one Jewish friend did he have." She was right. To me, that was the norm. I learned to deal with it in my own way. Like my father, I made friends and ignored their occasional comments. I learned to take the hand I was dealt and make the best of it. Maybe that is what Dad wanted. Maybe he thought it was an important lesson. It is important to know when to pick your fights and when to let things pass. I learned to take so many lemons and make so much lemonade that I hope I never have another glass.

I continued to discuss the nature of God with my father over the years. I found religion to be a fascinating subject. Like war, it often showed the best and the worst side of humanity. It lifted people to dream of a better world, and it caused them to hate one another over their differences. I liked Jewish history because it was a thread that wove through world history. Jews acted as witnesses to the barbarity and the great forward strides made by Europe. They even lived in China, India, and just about everywhere else at some point. They were loyal subjects of the countries in which they lived; they worked, paid taxes, and fought in the armies. They fought with the Visigoths against the Moors in Spain, and they fought with the Moors against the Hidalgos. They killed one another fighting in opposing armies. A Jew named Ernst Hess was Hitler's unit commander in World War I. A Jewish lieutenant, Hugo Gutman, recommended Hitler for the Iron Cross, and Gutman received the Iron Cross twice. One hundred thousand German Jews were in the German Imperial Service in World War I, out of a total population of 550,000. Ten thousand were volunteers. Twelve thousand German Jewish men died fighting for Germany in World War I. Thirty thousand were decorated. Seventy-five percent saw frontline service. Nineteen thousand were promoted. Two thousand were commissioned officers, and twelve hundred were medical officers. If you can believe it, estimates of as many as fifty thousand men of some Jewish background served in the Wehrmacht in World War II.

The English army had its own Palestinian brigades made up of Palestinian Jews in World War I and World War II. You can see their graves at the cemetery at Al Alamein in Egypt. Name a war and the countries involved. In most of them, you will find that the Jews fought on all sides. In the American Civil War, thousands of Jews fought and died on both sides. The first Jewish senator, Yehuda Benjamin, was from Florida, a slave state. He was known as "the brains of the Confederacy." He rotated through many of the top positions in the Confederate government. Without him, the government might have collapsed much sooner, and there would not have been enough supplies or weapons for the soldiers. The people turned on their government as the war turned against the South. Benjamin was referred to as Judas Benjamin in the newspapers. Yet for all that Jews did in the United States and in other nations, there is the insidious propaganda that lives on to this day: that they did not serve or belong to the countries they lived in.

My mother's beliefs were a little different. She used to say, "God is watching." I took that to mean that he did not control events, but that you would be judged for your own actions. My mother used Bible stories as allegories. Jacob and Esau was a repeated story of sibling rivalry. When

I told my mother how angry I was at my brother, she would tell me that I had to forgive and forget. When I asked why, she would say because he was my brother. One day I told her that was not good enough. She spun around from the sink in the kitchen, put her hands firmly on my cheeks, looked me in the eyes, and said, "That is the best reason in the world."

My father was busy dividing us, encouraging us to tell on one another. My mother did the opposite. She was not as cerebral as my father. She was simply the wisest person I knew. She kept us together, and she bent over backward not to play favorites or alienate us from each other. She had her complaints about Dad, but we had to be respectful and not say much. He treated her like a servant while extolling the great virtues of his sisters. He just said how wonderful they were and withheld any compliments for her except for her cooking. If anything, he was usually putting her down. It was just his way of dividing people. He liked pitting us against each other. That way he could tell who was the survivor, who was worthy, and who was found wanting.

At the age of eighteen, I decided against going to college right away. I ached to see the world and have an adventure of my own. I ended up backpacking around Israel, Turkey, Iran, Afghanistan, Pakistan, India, and Nepal. Later, I would travel again after college and visit Spain, Portugal, Morocco, Egypt, and Jordan. I was impressed with the power of Islam. It wasn't anywhere near as dangerous or hostile as it is today, but when the muezzin called and hundreds of people stopped to pray, you had to be impressed. The buses would stop at prayer time in the middle of nowhere, and the people would go outside and pray. From the Muslim world, I went to India and learned much about Hinduism—and Buddhism, in Nepal.

My aunt Halina, a very insightful person whom I could spend days talking to, once asked me what had I learned. How do you answer such a question? I learned so many things about life, many of which I cannot put down in words. I learned that people could express opinions about history, culture, and religion that are vastly different from our own and equally valid. As it concerns religion and culture, America was a land where we were sure that we were the greatest force for good in the world, sure in the rightness of our causes. It was a land where we projected our strength around the world, both militarily and economically; where we were taught so very little about other cultures, but everyone else in the world had to learn about us. It was where small nations had to stand by, helpless, while we projected our values and policies, and where Judeo/ Christian values were the right values.

Things became very confused for this American boy. It became clear that there were other opinions and viewpoints that were equally valid. Most importantly, they all followed their faiths with the same fervor. There was no right answer. The answer lies in where you live, what you are taught, and the culture you grow up in. I did learn that, like Judaism, Hinduism and Buddhism recognize that there are other ways to achieve enlightenment and salvation.

There are plenty of people who don't believe in God and many more who, like me, simply are not sure. If he does exist, he surely is not concerned about our petty, everyday concerns. How can you pray for help for yourself, as an individual, when there is so much mass suffering? Having finally met an avowed atheist, it occurred to me that she had as much faith that there was no God as any religious person had faith that there was. She had faith there was no afterlife. She had faith that all religion was an illusion. Maybe she was right. I just don't know how she could be any more sure of the negation of the divine than a religious person can be sure of its existence.

Much of this confusion could have been avoided if I had only stayed home. Sometimes, going out to see the world and discovering new ideas can cause confusion. It is just so much easier to stay close to your home, your roots, and feel sure about your country, your faith, and your ideals.

It would take many years for me to reconnect to Judaism. To me it was a duty, and continuing it for the sake of the past and all the suffering was insufficient reason to continue practicing something that had no meaning. In the 1960s and early 1970s, it was hard to hear a sermon that did not include the Shoah or some other period of suffering. That was our inheritance. It was not to sing in joy and praise the daily miracles that surround us. It became a religion defined by the Shoah. The passing of the survivors does not mean we forget, but it does mean that war is not "in our faces," and we no longer have to define ourselves as victims. I became like my father, dropping my son David off at the synagogue without going in. As he came close to the time of his bar mitzvah, I was required to come with him to services. I was ashamed that I could not remember the service or read a word of Hebrew and decided that I needed to reacquaint myself with my culture.

I met with the rabbi on weekday mornings, and we started off with elementary school Hebrew. Things came pretty quickly. As we had a part-time cantor, it was not long before I was helping to lead services. Soon I was reading haftaroth and, finally, the Torah itself. Did I start to believe in a God who saw our every move and decided if we were going to heaven or hell? No, I did not, and I doubt that I ever will. I did love the music, the congregational chanting, the calming effect of communal prayer, and the discussion of the weekly Torah portion and its meaning to us. It was a time to reflect upon my actions, thoughts, and behaviors. As a friend of mine said, it was a weekly moral tune-up.

When it came time for the bar mitzvah of my younger son, Jesse, my mother pulled out a plain-looking, small black-and-white tallit. The area around the neck was frayed, so a piece of light blue cloth was sewn to it for reinforcement. My mother told me it was my father's tallit that he wore at their wedding. Normally he would be buried in it, but my mother did not want to see it disappear from history. It was the one item, other than some pictures, that my family had from before the war. This was the tallit my grandfather Marcus had taken from the synagogue in Yoshkar-Ola. He kept it with him as he traveled with the Russian army. He gave it to my father to wear at the wedding because my father did not have one. He sewed the piece of cloth around the neck. My mother just could not stand the idea of it being buried. Jesse was not more worthy of this than the other grandchildren; it just happened that he was the last grandchild, and my mother had to make this decision now, or let it be buried. Of all the public speaking I have done, presenting Jesse with that tallit was my most important and proudest speech. When the subject of the Shoah comes up, people talk about murder, ghettos, and concentration camps. My mother's family always felt a little shunted to the side. Her family had a hard life. Hundreds of thousands of people in the Soviet Union died from starvation or the attendant diseases that come from hunger. My grandmother Rachael (all four foot nine of her) and my mother were the breadwinners in that family. That family stayed together. They never gave up hope. No one ever threw in the towel or took to alcohol or serious crime. That was their tradition, and that tallit gave me the chance to tell the story.

It took a long time, but the circle was closed, and that sense of alienation finally went away.

Ten

PINEWOOD DERBY

I stood in the jewelry store with the pieces of the pinewood derby car in my hands. I looked at my father, and a hard slap hit the side of my face. It had come out of nowhere. I had not disobeyed him or talked back. My face registered shock. I said nothing. I had absolutely no idea why I had been slapped. I was still trying to process the reality that I had been hit. It happened so fast that I was not yet sure it had happened. My father said that I looked at him like I wanted to kill him. I don't know where he learned to read minds, but he was wrong. I was angry and disappointed. His yelling at me was unfair, and I did not deserve to be hit.

I had tried to cut the shape with a saw but had made a mess of it. I had run out of patience. We were supposed to work on this together. I just wanted a relationship like other kids had with their dads. We didn't play sports together. We didn't throw a ball. We didn't do any projects together. I did not belong to the Cub Scouts, but they had a few extra kits left over, and one day the cubmaster dropped it off at our house. I thought this would be fun to do with my dad. He said we would do it together, but it wasn't happening. He was always too busy, even on Sundays.

At school during show and tell, boys would often get up and talk about going fishing, camping, or building things together with their fathers. I did not have those stories. I was jealous, so I made up stories, really good stories about catching big fish and playing football. I was always talking about my dad and all the great stuff we did together, but it was all a big lie.

This would be different. We would build this car and show off to the neighborhood what we could do together. We were different from the other families in the neighborhood. It was a blue-collar, non-Jewish neighborhood. At that time, many of the men had been in World War II or Korea. Most of them liked my parents and were loyal customers. Some of the men had seen the camps. Some had German backgrounds. Some were ashamed of what was done, even though it was not America's fault. My mother was pretty, upbeat, and had a cute accent, but my parents were still different. Outside of the business, they did not socialize much. As a child, I saw them as different from everyone else—and, of course, Christmas made it worse.

If you ever want to feel like an outsider, just imagine being a Jewish kid in a Christian neighborhood at Christmastime in the early 1960s. In school, we had a tree in every classroom. We spent class time stringing popcorn and berries with Christmas songs playing on a record player or over the school sound system. We did Christmas musicals. We learned the songs in music class, and we stood in the hallways singing Christmas carols. I never knew quite what to do. I sang along, but when the lyrics came to singing about Jesus as Lord and Savior, I didn't sing those words. It was my only form of resistance.

Once or twice, I actually had the guts to speak up to a teacher and tell them that I should not be doing this because it was not my holiday. Some of these teachers were Jewish themselves. Once I was even sent to the principal's office. They were very nice to me. They wanted me to know that they understood, but that the celebration of Christmas, Easter, and Saint Valentine's Day was secular, and in this country you had to go along with the majority. They explained the general secular values of these holidays.

Didn't they know we had our own holidays that taught values beyond baskets full of candy and lots of presents? Why weren't they teaching the other children that they were wrong in believing the simplistic equation that no Jesus equals no God, equals an eternity in hell? Didn't they know I could learn about the joy of giving without Christmas? Didn't they know I could learn about sacrifice without Easter?

So we were Jewish; my parents spoke with accents, and my father did not hang around shooting the breeze with other men. He didn't go bowling or belong to any organizations. He never went to a bar or tavern to hang out. If he didn't like coming home, he just worked longer hours. For a while, he worked two jobs. My mother took care of the store during the day while he worked at a factory. When he was done, he went to the store and fixed watches until eleven o'clock at night. He didn't gamble or follow the Phillies, the Eagles, or the 76ers. He didn't help out with the Scouts or come to watch a Little League game.

There was a small gang of juvenile delinquents led by one Larry Antenucci. They knocked over our trash cans until my mother waited for them and caught them. She was no wallflower, and she was not afraid of burly teenagers. She let them know what she would do to them, so they stopped. Sometimes they soaped up the windows on my father's store. It usually said "poor Jew" or some other intelligent comment. I got a bucket of soapy water and a sponge, stood on a ladder, and washed it off.

One evening Larry and his gang were hanging outside my father's store, knocking on the windows and trying to jam the door shut. Dad was only about five foot six. His back was stiff with arthritis, and he had curvature of the spine. His back problems came from the war. He walked very stiffly.

On that evening, he had enough. I guess like all parents, he ignored his own advice to his children and decided it was time to teach someone a lesson. He came out, reached up, grabbed Larry by the collar, and dragged him into the store and locked the door. We lived just a few doors down the street from the store. Gena came running in the house, saying Dad had Larry Antenucci and had slapped him around and knocked his head against a wall!

We all ran over to the store. There was a crowd of kids and teenagers outside. We could see through the window. Larry was rubbing the back of his head. My father was talking to him. My father thought he could reason with anybody. I am pretty sure he tried to get into Larry's head. He probably asked him why he felt so bad about himself that he had to go around picking on people who were different. Eventually they shook hands. Larry left the store and ran home. I was afraid of him. He still called my brothers and me Jews, but he left my parents alone after that.

Larry had two brothers. They also used the word "Jew" pretty often. Their father was a good customer and was very much a gentleman, especially to my mother. He did not seem like a man who taught his sons to speak like that. He even came to Scout camp and chaperoned for a few days. I never heard him say a bad word to anyone.

Still, I learned over time that kids learn by what their parents say or do at home. Teaching kids that other people are less worthy or using words like "kike," "spick," or "nigger" is how it gets passed on. I heard those words a lot when adults were talking. Children don't talk like that unless they learn it at home. They learn the words and the attitudes at home. My parents did not talk that way. They did not pick on any group, but they did know what made us different from the "goyim." Jews did not hang out in bars or gamble away the family's money. They came home after work. They did well at school. Most children would go to college. They became doctors, lawyers, actors, comedians, successful businessmen, and Nobel Prize winners. They valued family above all. They did not get divorced or abandon their families. They didn't have more children than they could support. They did not waste money on Christmas and go into debt for months afterward. They did not buy clothes at the holidays when prices were high. They handled their money responsibly. They worked as many jobs as it took to support the family and keep them out of poverty. They were so determined, stubborn, and single-minded that after two thousand years, they now had a country called Israel. They were soldiers and farmers, and they fought off armies many times their size. They made an agricultural success out of a desert.

My parents did not put down others, but they did something similar by indoctrinating us into believing that somehow we were better. It was not because of our race; it was because our religion and values were different. Our suffering made us stronger than others. We could take what the goyim dished out and be better. Discrimination was not necessarily a bad thing as long as it did not go too far. It kept us separate. It made us work harder. It drove us to succeed. There is a saying that as a minority, you have to learn to work twice as hard as others. My father did not think this was a bad thing. Learning to work harder for the same reward that others got made you stronger—maybe strong enough to survive the Nazis.

Dad had his own way of apologizing. He never actually said he was sorry. He just got nicer for a while. After he hit me, we stood in silence, glaring at each other. He was wrong, and he knew it. I was just a boy who wanted his father's help. He took the car, got a razor knife, and sat down on a stool. In ten minutes he carved a car. It wasn't like the other kids' cars. It didn't look like a Formula One racer. It looked like a racer out of the 1940s or '50s. The back was a rounded hump. It sloped down to the front. Joe wanted to be involved, so he painted it silver. It didn't have a bright color, it didn't have a plastic windshield, it didn't have a little person in the cockpit or a little steering wheel, and it didn't even have decals. It was kind of sad-looking. Dad didn't care about looks or being cool. He cared about performance. Dad, Joe, and I debated about what to do with the cockpit. Joe and I understood something about turbulence and drag from reading about airplanes. We covered the cockpit with scotch tape so there would be no turbulence and less drag.

The real engineering came from the wheels and axles. The axles were just small nails. The head of the nail was the hubcap. The nail went through the center of the wheel and was glued to the bottom of the car. Dad sat at his watchmaking bench with all the little tools and his tiny lathe. He sat with a magnifying loupe in his eye and gave it the same care as a watch, using all the fine feel and dexterity that made him a top watchmaker. On the wall in the back was his master's certificate from a school in Berlin. There was no better training in the world. He was afraid to hang it out front. He didn't know what people would think with all that German writing. You can be sure that none of the other dads had this kind of skill.

Dad took his tiny knife, honed it carefully by hand, and proceeded to cut any flash or irregularities off the plastic wheels. He polished the plastic on his lathe. Finally, he put the nails in his little lathe and used a narrow, fine-honing stone to bring the axles to a mirror finish. He put the axles through the wheels and into the slots that would hold them. He carefully checked each wheel so it was as tight as it could be without binding against the wood. He cut a square hole in the bottom and screwed lead weights in. He checked it carefully on his jeweler's scale and got it just to the legal limit.

While Dad couldn't be bothered with baseball games, swimming meets, or Scout meetings, he suddenly became very involved in this race. I came into the store on a Saturday (the busiest day of the week) and told Dad the race would be starting. He darted out from behind the counter. He could not run—his back was stiff as a board—but he could walk awfully fast. He looked like Charlie Chaplin with a longer stride. The racetrack was set up on the far side of the parking lot. He walked so fast that he actually beat me to it. We put our car on the table. The other kids joked about how it looked.

Dad was in the front of the crowd. He was shorter than the other men. He didn't wear slacks and a T-shirt. He always wore a jacket, tie, and white shirt. He always dressed like a European gentleman. He did not like the American fashion of walking around like a "schlepper."

The cars were weighed. The others were light. Ours was right on target. There were three heats and a final race. Every time our car ran the track, it zoomed ahead. In every heat and in the final race, it was first by a long shot. A woman yelled, "Check that car; it probably has a watch spring in it!" The crowd laughed, but they were amazed. The other fathers and mothers congratulated Dad. They crowded around to inspect this homely looking "vunder" car.

I rarely saw him this happy or proud, and I was darned proud of him. He picked up the car and held it up like it was the finest thing he ever made. Mom made a great dinner that night. We talked over and over about how our car zoomed ahead of the others. He kept the blue ribbon hanging from his bench for a few days. People came to the store and congratulated him. He got a kick out of explaining how he built the car. He had beaten the goyim again. In his head, I knew what he was thinking. He was a Jew. He was smarter than them.

I did not forget about the slap and the stress between us. I just knew that was part of having a relationship with him; and as a young boy, that was important to me. The car would come up in conversation for several years. He had a broad smile every time he talked about it. It took a long time for him to forget about that car, but I never did. I was happy we had finally done something together.

Eleven

The Jewelry Store Heist

Did I say in the last chapter that my father thought he could reason with anyone? He had done it with so many people who wanted him dead that he became fairly comfortable with the idea. When it came time to deal with an armed robber, the robber was putty in his hands.

It was 8:50 p.m. Ten minutes before closing. This was the classic time for a robbery. My parents knew this, but their guard was down. The two young men and one woman who came into the store were all nicely dressed. The men wore jackets and ties; the woman a dress. The woman and one of the men held hands and asked about engagement rings. The other man was a friend. They were also white. Had they been African Americans, my parents might have been more suspicious. My parents were not overtly racist. They had customers of all races. They got along well with everyone, and most people liked them. What can I say? They had become Americanized.

Harry, Joe, and I all worked in the store fixing electric shavers. I started at around ten years old, sharpening the shaving heads. At age thirteen, I started overhauling shavers. My father wanted to get people into the store. His store was at the end of the shopping center. The side faced a busy road that people used to get into and out of the city. There was no expressway from the suburbs at that time. He hung up a large sign: "Headquarters for All Shaver Repairs. All Makes and Models." We used to refer to the store as the headquarters. "How were things at head-quarters today?" my siblings and I would joke.

You had to go into the city to have a shaver repaired. My father's store was the only place in the suburbs that did it, so people were happy not to have to drive into the city, and my father charged less than the "authorized repair centers." My father was no dummy.

Instead of spending money on advertising, my father purchased a huge supply of old shavers and electric shaver parts from a man who was retiring from his fix-it shop. We rebuilt or reconditioned the old shavers and sold them used. As my father bought the stuff for a song, it was all profit and created a lot of goodwill.

We also butchered them for parts: wires, resistors, points, armatures, carbon brushes, cutting heads, and just about anything else you need-ed in a small electric motor. There were three major types of motors. Schick razors had a vertical spinning armature and used points. They operated in a similar fashion to a car's distributor. Norelco razors used a more traditional electric motor. The armature spun horizontally, and power was continually fed from the carbon brushes. Remingtons used a vibrating motor. These were the easiest to overhaul as they usually did not need disassembly; we would just clean out the dirt and sharpen the head. I learned to shape and gap the points, put an armature in a lathe, and hold emery paper against the copper ring to clean off the carbon; and most importantly, I learned to use a soldering iron. There were no manuals and no schools to teach us.

My father taught us the basics that were, to him, nothing more than common sense. First, you followed the "juice" or electricity. It did not matter whether it was a car, a washing machine, a vacuum cleaner, or a shaver. In most cases, you had a burned-out resistor or a loose wire. After that, you went to the mechanical components and observed how they should work. That was what watchmaking was about. There were so many different types of mechanical movements that all you could know was the basics and use your common sense to figure out the rest.

When my mother's vacuum cleaner broke down, my father told me to fix it. I had no idea what was inside. He told me to get a baking pan for muffins and slowly take the cleaner apart and put the parts in the pan, make sure I could reassemble every subassembly before moving to the next step, find the worn parts, replace them, and reassemble in the reverse order. My mother was amazed. I was amazed. My father told me you could learn to fix most things with just a little common sense. Of course, being able to fix things and eventually learning watchmaking would make me valuable if the Nazis came back. My mother also said I should learn in case I was ever injured, like my father, and could not work a normal job.

By age fourteen, during the summers, my father had me go into the city every Thursday to the jewelry district to take the jewelry repairs to the jobbers. Some just did polishing, and others just did stone set-ting or engraving or some other specific function. Dad would pack up a briefcase, write a to-do list, give me a few hundred dollars in cash and anywhere from a few thousand to twenty-five thousand dollars in jewelry, and send me walking a mile to the trolley stop, where I rode to Sixty-Ninth Street and took the elevated train into the city. I got off at Eighth and Market Streets and walked a few blocks to the jewelry district, where I did my rounds. I think back and wonder just how strange this seemed. I really think my father believed that no serious robber would bother a kid, because no one in his right mind would send a kid out with all that stuff. I gained a sense of responsibility, confidence, and independence other kids my age just did not have.

My father always told me how lucky I was that I had a job like this. Other kids were working in restaurants, making peanuts. I could fix two to three shavers in an hour at two dollars each. That was excellent mon-ey for a teenager at the time. The problem was that I was working with my father. It wasn't bad, provided he was in a good mood and not fight-ing with my mother. Otherwise, it could be miserable.

During the school year, I went in during the evenings and on Saturdays. This was a Friday evening. The perpetrators were out front, looking at engagement-ring sets. My father had matched sets in boxes in the case. My mother was helping him and talking to the young woman. My father locked the door at 9:00 p.m. I think they were waiting because they could hear me rambling around in the back. My father told me he should have suspected something because the robber tried to light his cigarette, but he was shaking so much that he couldn't. My father whipped out his trusty Zippo lighter and lit it for him. Dad attributed the man's nervousness to the thought of getting married. Given his own unhappy relationship, this seemed quite reasonable to him.

I was going through drawers in the back, looking for the right size of screwdriver. At 9:15 p.m. I walked out of the back and across the store to my father's watch bench, where I started looking through his drawers for the screwdriver. I never looked up. I was intent on what I was doing and did not notice anyone. I heard the words "Don't move." The words did not register at all. I kept looking through the drawers. He said it again, only louder: "Don't move." I looked up. He had what I believed was a military .45 semiauto pistol. I guessed this for three reasons. First, it was a drab olive military color; second, it was a flat slab; and third, the barrel looked like a cannon. I had seen police revolvers, and this was no .38. He had his hand on the grip and trigger; it was flat on the counter, and his other hand was on top of it. It was pointed directly at my mother's gut.

What the hell was this? I wondered. Was this some kind of joke? Nothing was registering. I started to walk forward, still trying to understand what he was saying and doing. Now he picked up the gun and pointed it at me. He told his friend to get me. His friend walked over, stepped behind me, and pinned my arms at my side. My parents were looking at me and suddenly everything registered. Sometimes you will hear that the police reported a victim was shot when they resisted. I am sure in many cases there was no resistance. The victim's inability to process what is going on may result in him failing to follow orders and prompt the perpetrator to pull the trigger.

There was no fear. Everything was surrealistically calm and moving at slow speed. I walked with the friend into the back. My parents calmly said,

"Don't hurt him." I calmly said, "Don't hurt them." He had me sit down in a chair in the back. He pulled out some clothesline. He tied my hands and feet. He was shaking. The rope was rotted green and loosely tied. I could have pulled it off at any time. I still had a fair-sized screwdriver in my hand. I thought of jabbing him with it, but the man with the gun on my parents was still in the front. Besides, at age sixteen, did I really know what to do? I could see him rifling through my mother's pocketbook. I thought what a slimeball this guy was, rummaging through my mother's pocketbook and stealing her cash. He went back out front. Should I get out of these ropes and slip out the back door? No, I thought. It could only cause trouble for my parents if he came back and I was missing.

I then heard my father reasoning with the robber. Remember when I said he thought he could reason with anybody? Could he even reason with a person who had a gun pointed at him? The robber had the power, because he had the gun, but when it came to the mental game, his gun might as well have been empty.

"Why are you doing this?" I heard my father ask. "Why do you want to risk going to jail?" I heard the robber tell him that he was out of work and had small children at home. In reality, he was a junkie. My father did not believe him, but he just wanted some kind of answer so he could say, "OK. I have insurance, and we will both make money." My father was intimating that he would make a large insurance claim and make money out of the deal. That would make them partners in crime instead of adversaries.

In fact, though my father had a safe and an alarm system, he did not have insurance for robbery. He did not want to pay the high monthly premiums, but he did not want the robber to know it. Instead, my father started to fill a bag with jewelry. He selected the least valuable items and told the robber they were worth a lot. When it came to the diamond engagement sets, my father pulled the open boxes out of the case one at a time. He turned the box toward him, fingered the rings, dropped them in his suit jacket pocket, snapped the box closed, and dropped it in the bag. It may seem to you that this was very risky, but he was very quick and smooth. I think he got a rush out of it. It was like being back in the war and living on the edge. He talked about smuggling food into the camp like it was a game. It was like the rush that a gambler gets. My mother knew what he was doing. She was holding the bag up high enough to block the robber's line of sight so my father could slip the rings into his pocket. She could spot someone outsmarting a thief any day of the week. They worked together without ever signaling each other. They may have done their share of bickering, but when it came to a threat to the family or business, they could work as a team without a word passing between them.

After handing the robber a bag full of cheap jewelry and empty plastic diamond ring boxes, my father told the robber that he should hurry and get out before someone saw him from the window and reported him. He was taking control of the situation. He was standing there with a pocketful of diamond rings. The robber put away his gun, shook my father's hand, and thanked him for his help. My father was shooing them out the door and promising not to say anything. I heard the door close. There was a rapid exchange of Polish. I pulled off the ropes and came out front. My parents were almost laughing. I really think they had a good time.

I had felt so calm during the whole affair. I walked outside. Now that it was over, I started to shake. I lit a cigarette, but it wasn't easy, the way my hands were shaking. If anyone asked me, I would swear it had taken an hour. I looked at my watch, but only about ten minutes had lapsed.

In law school, criminal procedure was a mandatory course. The professor was an inspirational, dynamic speaker. He graduated from a top-ten law school. He was about half my age, and he obviously knew little about the real world. One day he was talking about the constitutional procedures involved in identifying mug shots. I had heard enough at that point and told him about my real-world experience with the police and how they handled mug shots. The police came over to my house. They had a mug-shot book but showed me only two pages. I could not identify the robber. At the store, he was clean shaven, his hair was neatly combed, and he was wearing a suit. In the mug shots, everyone looked like a hardened criminal. In frustration, the detective pointed to a picture and asked me if this was the man. The man in the mug shot had long hair, a beard, and looked pretty mean. I said I could not tell if that was the right man. The detective pointed again and said that was the robber. I said, "OK. I guess that's him."

The detective pulled out a small black semiauto handgun. He said this was the gun. I told him it wasn't. "You said it was a forty-five, and this is a forty-five," the detective insisted. I told him again the gun was large and green. "It's a forty-five," he repeated. "This is the gun." I wasn't going to argue with the detective. They had gone to the robber's house. He gave up the jewelry and said he was a drug addict and wanted to go to rehab.

My father recovered his cheap jewelry and empty engagement-ring boxes. There was still a gun hanging around out there, and I was now fully baptized into the jewelry business. My father's mental manipulation of the robber was effective, and it was one of those skills he learned during the war.

Twelve

SCOUT CAMP

"Don't ever let them see you cry, no matter what happens. Don't ever give them the pleasure. If you cry, then they win, and they will play more tricks on you and tease you even more. Just go off somewhere on your own if you need to cry." My mother had to be one of the wisest people in the world. These were my mother's words to me at eleven years old as we packed my footlocker for Boy Scout camp. I had never been away from home for more than a weekend camping trip. "They will pick on you because you are new." She did not want to say that I would be picked on for being the only Jewish kid in the troop. We did not talk about that subject at home.

As children, we were expected to swallow it and then overcome. Of course, my parents were survivors. Their children must have somehow inherited this trait, but that was not the case. They could not seem to accept the possibility that we might not have been among those who made it. Some of us had physical ailments, and some of us were "too sensitive," as I was often told. I did not know until I went to camp that Harry had been teased every day, because he complained to the scoutmaster when he was picked on. They hounded him so bad he left the troop. Our lives were a constant assessment as to whether we had the skills to survive hard times.

It was a tough troop. The leaders did not like wimps. All of them were veterans of World War II or Korea and had no patience for complainers. I was expected to "rough it" and "suck it up." I was shocked later when we moved to another suburb, and I was reprimanded for pulling tricks on the younger scouts. They made me feel like a real roughneck who did not belong. My first troop was relatively small. It was small because they drove out the weaklings and complainers, but a genuine "esprit de corps" developed. At camp, there were games and competitions between troops. We did extremely well in competition with the larger troops. Larger troops were broken into patrols that were always in competition with one another. When it came time to pull together, they did not know how. Our troop did not have that problem. There were only two patrols, but we did everything as a troop.

At camp, I shared a tent with Johnny Antenucci. He was Larry's younger brother. Larry was the leader of a "gang" in the neighborhood who was always picking on my family because we were Jews. Johnny wasn't a bully like his brother, but he shared some of the same traits. He also had a short fuse. We got along OK because we shared a tent, and we were both rookies. We came back to our campsite after working on a merit badge, and our footlockers were hanging up in a tree. I laughed and shimmied up the tree, tied a rope to the handle, threw the rope over a limb, and lowered my footlocker to the ground. Johnny started screaming and crying. He climbed up the tree, but he was so frustrated, he just cut the rope that held up the footlocker and let it crash to the ground, where it broke open and spilled everything. He fell from the tree and just sat there, crying. The older boys got a real kick out of Johnny's reaction. I helped him put things back together. At times we were friends, but at other times I did not like him very much. Still, he was my tent mate and fellow rookie.

I got used to inspecting my tent for booby traps every time I came back to the campsite. The bottom of my sleeping bag might be wet, and I wouldn't know until I went to bed and my feet got wet and cold. I always checked my bag. If it was wet, I hung it out to dry without ever saying a word. Sometimes we would come back to camp, and the contents of our tent were perfectly set up in the middle of the campsite. I would force a laugh and quietly put everything back. Johnny would get pissed off and yell. He couldn't seem to get it through his head that this was what gave pleasure to the older boys, who already had a lot of merit badges and were bored at camp.

Johnny did not have a mother who was wise and could give him the kind of advice that my mother could. The rumor was that Johnny's mother was in a psychiatric hospital. During one of my inspections, I noticed that the legs of my bed closest to the edge of the floor were just hanging out of the tent. I immediately fixed the bed and said nothing. I did not realize that it was an act of sabotage. I just thought it was my fault when I made my bed, so I did not think to check Johnny's bunk. Those watching were disappointed. Johnny came back a few minutes later, flopped into his bed, and crashed through the side of the tent, banging his head against a small tree. He screamed and cried and held his hand against the side of his head. The boys laughed louder than I had ever heard them before.

At about that time, the boys stopped playing tricks on me. They admired me for not complaining and began including me in the group. I became a sort of mascot. I was the Jewish rookie scout who could take it. Johnny became jealous and hostile toward me, but I ignored it. There were still two older scouts who pushed me around and just didn't like me. They were bullies, and it was obvious they came from homes where unkind words about Jews were bandied about. They didn't like the idea that I was not getting the full rookie treatment right to the last day of camp. It was worse because I was a Jew and wasn't really one of them. The other boys stood up for me and forced them to leave me alone.

I played the trumpet at home. The troop had a bugle, and I became the bugler. I learned "Reveille," "Taps," "Call to the Colors," and "Retreat," with a little boogie-woogie thrown in. Every evening before dinner, the entire camp assembled in full uniform and stood at attention for the flag-lowering ceremony. It was a time for quiet, solemnity, and respect. Every day a different bugler played "Call to the Colors" and "Retreat" as the flag was lowered and folded. Some of them were not very good, but no one would ever say anything. Some of the guys thought I should give it a try. It was a little frightening for an eleven-year-old. I practiced, and one night I got up there and did it. I didn't miss a note, and they were all nice and crisp.

I had brought honor to the troop. I got pats on the back and a firm handshake from the scoutmaster. I found friendship and closeness in the troop. It was the only place in my youth where I felt a closeness and bonding with others, and our ages made no difference. We ranged from eleven years old to sixteen. We rode our bikes together, helped one another, taught skills to the younger ones, and protected one another. In the warm weather, we had our weekly meetings outside in a park, where we built bonfires. During the camping trips, we also built bonfires—the bigger the better—and we sang scout songs. Perhaps it was not as exciting as my father's time in the Zionist youth organization, but I understood the appeal and camaraderie that came with belonging. The Scout leaders became surrogate fathers. They never said a word about Jews and would tolerate no jokes from the other boys. Once you showed them that you could "take it" from the others and not complain, you were no different from the others.

All the adults knew my parents. They liked them, they respected them, and they admired them for what they had gone through. They watched them build a local business and treat their customers with honesty and respect. When Dad first opened the store, it was the end store closest to the main road. Without that location, he would have no visibility from the traffic and would not have survived. There was room for one more store on the end, and the landlord decided to build. My father needed that location but could not afford it, not only because of the rent but also because he would have to invest in merchandise to fill the space. No bank would give him a loan in those days. A customer who liked my father loaned the money to him.

His last name was Lilac, and that was how he was referred to. Lilac had fought in the war. His background was German, and he even had relatives who fought in the Wehrmacht during World War II. He insisted my father take a no-interest loan from him. My father had no collateral to guarantee the loan and was not sure he would succeed and be able to pay back the loan.

Lilac was a chain-smoking, loud, coarse, opinionated man, and you could not say no to him because he would never give you the chance. I do not think he had many friends at all. Perhaps he liked my father because my father would patiently listen to him while he worked at his watch bench and nod his head in agreement when Lilac would go on one of his tirades against antiwar, long-haired, protesting, lazy, no-good, disloyal young people; communists; and other malcontents. I did not care for him much, as I was growing up into an antiwar, long-haired malcontent. I did admire him for the respect he paid my parents. Lilac truly believed my mother and father were the kind of people who built this country, and they were the kind of people this country was built for. In that respect, I had to agree with him.

To fill the new space, Dad added a lot of giftware, electronics, and greeting cards. When the Scouts came in for a Christmas present or their first gift to a girl, my parents would charge them little or trust in their honesty to pay them over time. They tried to make sure everyone was happy. They knew the families from the neighborhood. They knew who could afford to spend more and who couldn't. They charged different prices to people. The poorer ones got a better discount. In my father's mind, he was being fair, even though he charged different prices to different people for the same item. My mother knew who my friends were, and I had told her who had helped me at camp and protected me from the bullies. She always took special care of them. At Christmastime, my parents made sure all who came in got something they could be proud to give, whether they were adults or teenagers. No one walked out empty-handed, even if they had to extend credit, and the customers appreciated it. It didn't hurt us kids around the neighborhood, either, to have parents who could help them.

My parents taught me the importance of a good reputation, especially as a Jew in a non-Jewish world. My parents taught me to be independent, to be a go-getter, and not to rely on others for help. I was told not to look for justice or fairness in this world. If you got it, that was great, but don't go expecting it. I was told to help myself, to not be shy, and to open my mouth and ask for help when I needed it. By teaching self-reliance, they were more American than most Americans I knew. On some Sundays when I was bored and watching television, my father would draw a map for me and tell me to ride my bike somewhere, usually two or three miles away. Sometimes it was to an old neighborhood, a bowling alley, or a movie theater where I could spend a few hours. If I got lost, I was told to ask for directions. At the end of the day, I gave him a report on my activities. It was all part of the survival training.

He taught me how to sew a button and darn a sock. These are simple things to us. You get Mom to sew your button, and you throw away the sock with the hole. He thought it was important to learn these skills because in the concentration camps, a button was very important in keeping your shirt or coat closed in the wintertime. Socks could not be easily replaced unless you took them off a dead person, and he was too afraid of disease to do that. Socks were important for your feet when you wore wooden shoes, and very important in the winter.

At Scout camp, I showed other Scouts how to sew buttons on uniforms so the troop would not lose points at inspection. I showed them how to darn their socks when they got holes. No one had a large selection of those green Scout socks. I would put a flashlight in the sock. I would stretch out the hole a little and start weaving the thread. I did this for the boys whether I liked them or not. I did it for those who were nice to me and those who weren't. I made friends with these simple gestures, and I became just another helpful Scout and not simply the Jewish kid.

I have two more Johnny stories. My first year in the Scouts would not be complete without them. Every new camper bought a moccasin kit from the camp store. The leather was bonded to hard rubber soles, and all the holes were punched. Beyond that, you stitched everything together according to the instructions and then went to the leather-working site and decorated them with your own initials and any other design you could think of. Someone went into our tent while we were out and punched a few extra holes in Johnny's moccasins. When he started work on them, he became confused. He was not very good at reading or following instructions in the first place. I tried to help him. I compared his moccasins to the instructions and found they did not match. By this time, Johnny had a lot of resentment toward me and didn't want my help. It wasn't long before Johnny was yelling, crying, and slamming the moccasin sole against his forehead. After sewing, unsewing, and re-sewing several times, punctuated by yelling, crying, and more slamming against his head, he finished the moccasins, but they were the saddest-looking moccasins in camp, and he gave untold hours of enjoyment to the Scout troop.

Johnny also had an obsessive habit of honing his knife and throwing it. He was criticized, and the older scouts and adults warned him. All the scouts had some obsession with their knives. Between knives, axes, hatchets, and fire, it still amazes me that we came out with so few injuries. Most had some kind of wound, but Johnny was heading into uncharted waters. A few times, he threw his knife and nearly hit someone, including me. One day we were sitting on the picnic table, shooting the breeze. Johnny sat there on the top of the table with his feet on the bench, repetitively throwing his knife into the bench. No one paid attention to Johnny until the howling erupted. Johnny had thrown the knife through his foot, the sole of his shoe, and into the wood. Blood flowed out from the wound, down his shoe, and onto the bench. He pulled out the knife and threw it down. He was fortunate. The blade did not cause any permanent damage. Johnny was sent home early from camp. He was just too dangerous. There were only a few days left, but the troop had lost its favorite form of entertainment.

When I came home from camp, I had a million stories to tell. My parents were very proud that I had jumped into the flaming pit of prejudiced gentiles and came out happy and with new friends. To them I was truly an American child: fitting in with the others, being part of a patriotic organization, wearing a uniform, taking my mother's advice, ignoring the bigots, realizing there were good people who liked me for the content of my character and couldn't care less about my ethnic heritage. Through my siblings and me, my parents were creating a life they could not have dreamed of as children and, as destiny would have it, would not have come about were it not for the war. For me, it was possibly the happiest time I had as a child.

My older son, David, joined the Scouts. I helped out as a chaperone. It was my way of paying back. He would also attend summer camp at Resica Falls in the Pocono Mountains. I came up for a week to help out the scoutmaster. I walked around the camp for the first time in thirty years. I could not believe how small it had gotten. The parade ground, the mess hall, and the trails had all gotten smaller. I started to choke up a little when I began to realize how long it had been and how fast the time had gone by.

Once I got over those early emotions, I settled in. How I enjoyed the laughter from the boys. Most were at an age where their voices had not yet changed. When they laughed, I could hear my own boyhood laughter. I could even hear Johnny and me laughing together. The younger ones needed to be taught not to pick on the weaker or "weirder" ones and to try to integrate everyone into the group. I realized the concept of "rookie treatment" was always wrong. It hurt and excluded too many. I enjoyed the young teenagers. I made sure they spent time helping and teaching the younger ones. Their voices had changed, and they thought they were men. They went back into the woods and smoked cigarettes and drank beer. They thought they were clever, but I had a good idea of what was going on. I would go back to their little campsite when they weren't around and find their cigarettes under a carefully crafted pile of rocks—the same type of hiding place I would have used. I checked their tents and found the twelve packs of soda with the trace of glue around the opening tab of the cardboard. I pulled back the tab and removed the outer layer of sodas, only to find the beer cans that I expected to find. I trashed the evidence of their crimes and assured them I would tell no one if they discontinued these illicit activities.

Suddenly I became "cool." I also kept plenty of treats in my foot-locker that I would toss out to the boys when they seemed bored. "You're all right, Mr. Bruner!" I had my guitar with me. The older boys wanted to hear "oldies." I was surprised at how many of them knew the lyrics. They would crowd into my tent, eat candy, and sing oldies. They did as much for me as I did for them.

After breakfast, I would chase the boys off to their merit-badge classes. I put a folding chair out by the fire pit, got a book out, spread popcorn on the ground nearby, and put a pot of water on the fire. I sat very still and waited for the animals to come into camp: the birds, the squirrels, and the chipmunks. They came cautiously, slowly closing in. They entered the tents and scrambled around until the head scout came walking into camp. He was from England. He was seventeen years old, and it was his job to walk to all the campsites, inspect, and fill out an inspection report. We sat and had tea and talked about scouting and the differences between England and America. We talked history, the Revolution, and the Civil War. He just seemed to want to know as much as he could about the United States. He came every day, and every day I had tea ready for him, and we had a nice long chat. It didn't hurt as far as going easy on the inspection reports.

At first glance it seemed everything was the same, other than the fact that there were a lot fewer boys in scouting, and there were a number of women scoutmasters. The boys were still the same. They were a little more worldly, but they still craved the companion of other males and men to talk to, men who weren't their fathers and who were likely to keep their confidences.

Thirteen

MY SECOND BIRTHDAY: MATES BRUNER

It was the night of April 22, 1945—what I like to call my second birthday. I am not a drinker, but every April 22 after that I would have a few shots of slivovitz and some grain alcohol. I was lying on a bench in a police station, using my wooden shoes as a pillow. I was in a room with two policemen who were playing cards at the table and drinking from a bottle. I did not even know the name of the town at the time. It was warm, and it was raining. It was the kind of night that would put you to sleep, but I could not sleep, and the guards were going to be awake all night. I bit my lip and kept shaking my head. The air hissed as I expelled it from my pursed lips. This could not be happening, not now, not when I was so close to the end of the war. It was my destiny to make it through. I had been struggling for five and a half years. I had been fighting for my life in camps for three and a half years. I was sick, weak, and oh so weary of the struggle. How easy it would be to give in and die. The Allies were so close, and now I would be shot in the morning. I was out of miracles. I had come all this way, and now I would end up in an unmarked grave, and no one—no one—would know where I was buried or how I died.

Late in 1944 I was transported from Plaszow to Sachsenhausen near Berlin. I was still a valuable worker. The Germans still needed watchmakers, and I had become quite skilled at making my own tools and improvising spare parts from tiny pieces of metal. Because I was still young, my eyes were sharp, and I could often work without a magnifier. Sachsenhausen was a show camp, though many inmates would dispute that, depending on their experiences. At first, it was for political prisoners, Polish intelligentsia, and local Jews. The Red Cross would come and see what a great place it was and how the Nazis were not so bad. As the war continued, and the Germans were retreating from eastern Poland, there was a lot more killing of Poles and Russian prisoners. I was still in a part that was the show camp. I was in the watchmaking shop with a professional bench and tools. The shop was set up in a section of the hospital where wounded German soldiers were sent. I had decent (for a prisoner) clothes, soap, food, and I was even paid funny money that I spent in a little German tavern where I could get potato salad and beer. It was a farce, but at least I was doing all right for the moment, considering the murder that the Nazis were committing on a daily basis. I didn't need to hustle. All I needed to do was follow the rules.

It didn't last. Every camp had kapos in the barracks to watch over the prisoners and keep them in line. They were often German criminals or other German-friendly persons with criminal, sadistic, or violent backgrounds. They were hard and mean. They took a cut of every illicit thing you did, or they would report you. At Sachsenhausen I had a German kapo who wanted me to fix a watch for someone as a favor. I told him I couldn't. They inspected my work during the day, and if I were caught working on unauthorized personal jobs, I would be punished. The kapo made it clear that if I didn't fix the watch, he would make up a story about me and get me shot. I took the watch. I worked on it, and sure enough, an officer came by, and there was no work ticket. I was told to get up from my bench and go outside. I was given a backpack full of rocks and told to walk in a circle, and if I stopped or fell, I would be shot.

I started marching in a circle. It was still early in the day. I would march all through the day without food or water. I had been around long enough now to know how this day would end. They were just waiting for me to collapse so they could shoot me as an example to others. Everyone had to know that shooting was not so easy. Some would like to die quickly. The Nazis wanted us all to know that you were going to suffer before you finally begged for death.

The sun was getting lower in the sky. The commandant walked by. There was only one thing to do. I left the circle, marched up in front of him, and said, "Herr Commandant. The kapo forced me to fix a watch against my will. I am a Jew, and anyone can step on me and crush me under his heel." Now I was either going to be shot, or a miracle would happen.

The commandant told me to drop the pack and go back to my barracks. I would be shipped out the next day to a punishment camp. Some people might think the commandant did me a favor. You might think he got soft, and somewhere deep down there was a small drop of humanity in him. Don't be fooled. I knew what I was doing. I was going to be shot, so if the commandant was in a bad mood, that would happen anyway. Nobody wants to think of himself as a bad person, especially a Nazi. His victims simply did not understand why they had to be eliminated for the greater good. How could he expect them to understand? They were *untermenschen*. Certainly no member of the SS was in any doubt about what he was doing. The commandant could afford to do me a favor. He knew all Jews were going to die, so he could afford to be kind. He knew he wasn't giving me my life; he knew that all he was doing was giving me some time. I understood clearly what he was thinking, and he did what I expected. He could tell himself what a good man he was. He could go home to his wife, have dinner, and tell her about his act of kindness today. Tomorrow he would go back to having Russian prisoners shot in the back of the head and torturing Polish intellectuals. Today he was a man with a heart, a real nice guy.

I get a little tired of hearing about good Nazis. The only one I knew about was Oskar Schindler. He was one of the rare few to actually help Jews get through the entire war at risk to his own life. The rest might help you. Maybe they could save you from a certain work detail. There was no personal risk involved. They did not violate orders. They might even get your whole family into a better camp or an easier job, but every one of them was indoctrinated to believe that all the Jews would be killed eventually. What did it matter to them if today they saved someone? Did it really matter to them if you were the first Jew murdered or the last?

It mattered to the Jew who sincerely hoped the favor would help him outlast the war. No member of the SS was forced to serve in the camps. Some could not stand it. Anyone who asked for a transfer to serve in a military capacity was accommodated. Any Nazi who served in the camps was glad to do so. It was preferable to fighting for your country. The food was better. You lived in a barracks and slept in a bed. All you needed was to be the kind of person who found your own safety and comfort preferable to risking your life, even if it meant passively or actively being part of one of the most barbaric, cruel, brutal, sadistic group of murderers to walk the planet.

I didn't exactly know what a punishment camp was. Other than death, exactly how could I be punished any more than I had been already since 1939? The next day I got on a train. I did not know the name of the camp or where it was. I don't even know if the camp had a name. When I arrived, I was brought inside a cement building and never saw the light of day. In one room, I slept on a cement floor with Russian prisoners. For fourteen hours a day, we poured pig iron into floor sand-molds for grenades. It was hot; the red molten iron splashed when it hit the molds, and we had no protection of any kind. There was no ventilation, so we breathed in the fumes from the molten metal.

A meal was one loaf of bread for three men, and a little butter and soup made from boiled potato peels. You can believe it when I say that bread was cut *very* carefully. Every day we rotated who would cut the bread and who would pick the first piece. Whoever cut always took the last piece. It was obvious we would eventually die, but that was not what bothered me. In my head was the constant calculation and recalculation of time. How much time could I get from the given circumstances? Would it be enough time to make it to the end of the war?

Once again I was given a dilemma. The Russians told me that they purposefully did not clean out the inside of the castings completely.

In certain areas that you could not readily see with a cursory inspection, they left bits of sand or did not clean out the flashing completely. This would prevent the grenade from exploding. As I did not want the Germans to kill me, I did a thorough job of cleaning out the castings. The Russian prisoners took me aside and asked me what I was doing. "Look here, Abramchik. These grenades are used to kill our comrades. If you help us sabotage the grenades, the Germans might find out, and you might get shot. If you don't sabotage those grenades, you will definitely have an accident and end up in a pool of molten iron."

My instincts told me to follow orders. We had guards, and I doubted the Russians could carry out their threat. However, they might be able to, and there was something else involved. Up until now, I had spent every waking moment trying to stay alive. The work I did was never critical to the war effort one way or another, so I never thought much about it. Here, the Russians were on the right side. These were munitions and had a direct effect on the battlefield.

Certainly, grenades would not decide the course of the war, but why should I help kill anyone who was trying to help me by ending the war as soon as possible? We weren't going to live very long in this place; that was certain. If I had to die before the end, then at least I had a chance of helping someone who deserved my help. Like the Russians, I started sabotaging the grenades. The Russians were appreciative. They still called me Abramchik, but sometimes when the bread was cut and the crumbs lay on the borderline, they would sweep them over to my side. You couldn't do much more for a person in those circumstances. There was something you had to like about the Russians. If they liked you, they would give you the shirts off their backs or their last crumbs of bread. If they didn't, well, you could end up in a pit of molten iron.

The inexorable march of the Russians continued, and the Nazis kept retreating. This factory was being abandoned. Most of the Russians were shot. My papers still said I was valuable, so I was shipped out to Bergen-Belsen. By now, I had trouble doing any manual labor. I was just a bunch of skin stretched over bones. All my joints stuck out, connected to one another by thin sticks. I could not remember when I had last washed. My teeth hurt. My gums bled. No matter what position my body was in, I was in pain, because I was resting on bone. It was now March 1945. When the bombs were not dropping, the leaflets were. The Allies were so close. I had lost faith in the existence of God, but now I prayed for the strength to make it to the end.

I hoped that Bergen-Belsen would provide the same chances for survival as Plaszow. I was wrong. The camp was filled way beyond capacity. There wasn't enough work. There wasn't even any food. When I arrived, I was given a spoon for the thin potato peel soup I was supposed to get. I was given nothing for three days. I was sure this was the end. I could barely move. At the end of the third day, I sharpened the end of my spoon against a rock to a sharp point. The next morning at assembly, I had every intention of killing at least one German before I died. My name began with a B, so I would be near the front row. I would jump the guard and jam the point of my spoon into his throat.

I did not want to end up like so many others, a dead body lying on the ground. Every day the bodies littered the camp. People would be walking and then just collapse. If I had to die, I wasn't just going to collapse. I was going to take at least one of those bastards with me.

In the morning, the guards brought soup and bread. I was going to live another day, and so was the guard. Eventually, they put me in the watchmaking shop. I took a small pair of wire cutters and strapped it to my inner thigh. I hoped that somehow I would be able to escape. I knew I would never make it to the end of the war in this place.

The news was out at morning assembly. The Germans needed volunteers to go to Hamburg to help clean up the mess. The Allies bombed Hamburg day and night. Hamburg was a rail center, and the lines had to be fixed. Thousands of prisoners ran toward a long table where names were being taken. There were no lines, just a crush of stinking, filthy humanity. The guards were beating us with their truncheons, trying to keep order. I raised one arm to take the blows from the guards and used the other to push through the crowd toward the table. So many were weaker than me that when I pushed them, they just fell over. I clawed my way through the crowd, punching and kicking my way toward that table. I prayed I would get there before they stopped taking names. I was an animal now. Nothing mattered except getting to that table. My arm was so numb from the blows of the truncheons that I couldn't even feel the pain. I made it to that table, scratched up and bloody, but I got my name on that list. We were immediately put on the train for Hamburg.

When the train door opened, I knew that finally there was some justice in the world. There were hardly any buildings standing. The train rails looked like modern sculpture, twisted and scattered. The train cars were strewn around as though it were a messy child's playroom. Civilian bodies lay everywhere, and the smell was as bad as Bergen-Belsen. Smoke still came from the ruined buildings. The air was black and sooty. The soot came from anything that would burn, including people. The Allies were using napalm. I was told it was like a jelly. If it got on your skin, it burned; if you tried to rub it out, it went deeper into your skin and burned. If you hid in a cellar, it seeped through the cracks and burned everyone it touched. If you didn't die from fire, you died from smoke. If you didn't die from smoke, you died from asphyxiation, because the fire engulfed the city and sucked up all the oxygen. We went to work clearing rubble, straightening out rail lines, and putting them back in place. We carried the charred bodies of men, women, and children, even babies, and piled them up. We doused the piles with gasoline and set them on fire.

At the end of the day, we were taken to the submarine base. It was safe. It was below ground, protected by several feet of concrete and rubber. There were beds and canned food. The guards were German soldiers and not SS. They let us have what we wanted. They did not care. They were not fanatics. So many soldiers had already lost family to the bombings. For many, their homes had been destroyed; and for some, their families were gone. They had only one goal: to survive long enough to be captured by the Western Allies. They had no illusions as to what the Russians would do. They were the victors, and they were killing, pillaging, and raping the women and girls. The Soviets were headed for Berlin. The Western Allies were heading for the ports, the industrial centers, and the areas where there were raw materials. If they could stay in the north, the British would be the occupiers.

We ate well and slept on comfortable beds. We had canned meat, vegetables, and wine. We could not sleep because the bombing raids went on all night. The beds were too comfortable to get any rest. The food made us vomit and gave us diarrhea. There was nothing wrong with the food, but our stomachs had shrunk, and our organs were not used to processing anything more nutritious than a potato. When the Allies found starving refugees, they gave them lots of food. Many of them died from this kindness. It took a little while before the soldiers were given orders not to feed the refugees unless there was a doctor supervising. Above us, the German civilians were burning, but we were safe. I had no hate for the civilians. They were suffering like the rest of Europe. I was just glad it was not me who was suffering at the moment. I had done my fair share.

In the morning, we came out, and Hamburg looked the same as it had the day before. We did the same work as the day before. Burning bodies had become routine. The dead around me meant nothing now as long as I was alive. This routine went on for a few weeks. The food was helping me put on some weight, and I was getting stronger, though I was still a shell compared to what I looked like before the war.

One day, the guards told us that what we were doing was of no use anymore, and they put us on a train back to Bergen-Belsen. Once again, I believed it was over for me. I would die in Bergen-Belsen, and the war was almost over. If only I had a little more time.

The train creaked along, stopping for long periods. The stations along the way were backed up. During the night, we pulled into a town. The air raid sirens went off. The guards left with the doors locked and ran to the shelters. I had been talking to two Russian prisoners. They were brothers, and they wanted to escape. The others in the car were

113

too afraid. They were sheep, and they did not care if they were going to be slaughtered. I cared, and I was not done trying to make it through alive. I still had my pair of wire cutters. I stood on the shoulders of one of the Russians. There was a small window near the roof, covered with barbed wire. I cut the wire away, broke the glass, and jumped out, holding my wooden shoes so I would not make much noise when I hit the ground.

I jumped under the train wheel for cover until I could see what was going on. The Russian brothers landed and started running. I wanted to yell at them, but I was too afraid of making any noise. I lost sight of them in the darkness. I was alone now, and scared. I ran from the train station. I had no idea what direction to run in. I didn't know where I was or what I should do next. I came upon a building that looked like a barracks. There was a line of people shuffling in. I could hear them speaking Polish. They were foreign laborers brought to Germany. I went up to the line and asked for help. We learned how to talk like a Catholic when we needed to. I blessed the Holy Mother of God of Czestochowa for bringing me to my kinsmen. How strange that in the name of God they would not help a Jew, but for the sake of the Black Madonna, they would help me.

A few men brought me in. There was a long hallway with doors that opened into rooms full of bunk beds. One man walked me to the end of the hall and opened the door. Then he told me to crouch behind the door so that I was wedged between the door and the back wall. He came back with a bowl of soup. I ate as quietly as I could.

I could hear the footsteps coming slowly down the hall. A hand curled around the edge of the door, and slowly the door was pulled back. There was a German policeman looking down at me, crouched on the floor with a soup bowl in my hand. "What are you doing here? Who are you? Show me your papers!" I told him I had no papers. He grabbed me and walked me to the police station. The phone rang. There were prisoners who escaped from the train. "We have one," the policeman said. He hung up the phone. He walked me to a room and called for two guards. "You will be shot in the morning," he said and turned away, closing the door.

How could I have come this far only to be arrested now? I knew that if I had gone back to Bergen-Belsen, I would die there. I cursed at God for letting me come so far only to be killed now. I knew what Moses must have felt like when he viewed the Promised Land but could not go in. I bit my lip and shook my head back and forth. This could not be happening. I didn't know what time it was, but it was nearing dawn. The sky was beginning to lighten, and I could hear a bird. I looked over at the guards, and they were asleep, their heads resting in their arms on the table.

This must be a dream. I could not believe they were really asleep. I got up slowly, holding my wooden shoes. I walked oh so softly across the floor. I had to get by the guard whose chair was pushed back near the wall. I sucked in what little gut I had left, my stomach rubbing against the chair and my back rubbing against the wall. I got to the door, exited, turned the knob, closed the door softly, and slowly released the knob. There was a key in the latch. I began to turn the key and lock the guards in, but when it started to click, I wondered what the hell I was doing. I stopped turning the key and started down the hallway. I was afraid to run and afraid to walk at the same time. I started to walk very fast but tried to act nonchalant. I must have looked like Charlie Chaplin as I left the building and walked quickly down the road out of town, hoping I was invisible.

After a few kilometers I came upon a farmhouse. I walked up to the door, swallowed hard, and knocked. A middle-aged farmer came to the door. I told him I was hungry and asked if he had any work. He looked me over. His eyes went from my head down my body to my wooden shoes and back up. His wife came to the door and stared at me. They weren't fooled. My head was nearly shaved, I was wearing rags, I weighed next to nothing, and I spoke German with a foreign accent. It was obvious I had escaped from somewhere. He took me into the barn. His wife brought me soup filled with vegetables, potatoes, and bread.

The farmer pushed aside a hay pile and started digging a trench. He told me to get in the trench and pushed the hay over it. I know why he had done this. If anyone was looking for me and shot into the haystack, I would be below ground level. The police did come looking for me. They told the farmer that some concentration-camp prisoners had escaped from a train last night. The farmer told them he had seen no one. I cannot be sure of the farmer's motives. Perhaps he was just a good man who would have helped me anytime. Maybe he was feeling guilty at the end, as many Germans did. He might even have been self-serving. Having helped save an enemy of the Reich could be important if the Allies wanted retribution. It did not matter any longer. He helped me, and I would never forget it. The next day he put me to work chopping wood. I was so glad to be in the fresh air.

Znijmy znijmy mamie drzewo
znijmy w prawo znijmy w lewo
by mamusia nasza miala
by nam zupy zgotowala
znij-my znij-my-siups!

We cut—we cut—some wood for Mother,
we cut to the right—we cut to the left—
so that our mother can cook some soup,
the soup that is so good,
we cut—we cut—whoop!

This is a Polish children's song. My father sang it to me long ago. He bounced me on his lap and swung my arms back and forth in a sawing motion.

I was in a state of euphoria. I needed no alcohol. The war would be over in days, maybe a few weeks at most. I sang this song out loud as I cut the wood. I was going to sing this song to every child, grandchild, and great-grandchild who would ever sit on my lap. I was feeling healthier already. I was alive. I had been tested, and I was not found wanting. I never succumbed to dysentery, typhus, diphtheria, or any number of other diseases. I had made it. I had been through the fires of hell. The devil was dead, but I was alive.

Fourteen

RUGALACH: SAM BRUNER

Consider the subtleness of the sea;
how its most dreaded creatures glide under
water, unapparent for the most part,
and treacherously hidden beneath the loveliest tints of azure.

—HERMAN MELVILLE, *MOBY-DICK*

On some Sundays, my parents would pick us up from Hebrew school in Yeadon, Pennsylvania. We would drive down Market Street into Philadelphia, under the elevated train into the old Jewish neighborhood where the kosher butchers were. It was a different world for me. First we would go into the fish market. This wasn't like the grocery store. A Hasidic man with a bloody apron would take my mother over to the metal tank with the live carp swimming around. She would only buy fresh carp to make gefilte fish. She would nod her head, pointing to a fish, and speak to the man in Yiddish. He reached into the tank, grabbed the fish by the tail, swung it in a high arc, and slammed it down on his butcher's block. He would give it a good knock in the head with a wooden mallet and throw it on the scale. My mother would nod her head again. He brought the fish back to the block and gave it another whack or two.

Joe would grab my hand and take me to the back, where we could watch the fish being gutted. "Look at the eyes," Joe would tell me. The butcher would take a heavy knife, lay it on the fish's neck, and hit it with a wooden mallet. Joe was right. As the head slowly separated from the body, the eyes stayed open. Then came the gutting process. I did not know what the parts were, but it was an interesting process.

We would go to the butcher shop next, where my mother would buy the chickens. The heads were still on them. To be kosher, they had to have their throats cut quickly and cleanly with a special knife. They did not chop the heads off and let the bird flail around. Death was quick. In Judaism, that is the only acceptable way to kill. The butcher would take off the head and cut up the chicken for her. Back home she would throw everything into the pot to make her soup. I was a little grossed out by the yellow feet floating in the pot and would not eat the soup.

Soon we were at the deli. My parents bought golden-colored smoked whitefish. The heads were on them, so I definitely was not eating that. They also bought the traditional lox. It was a deeper color than Nova lox. It was heavier and very salty. They went on to buy more of my father's favorite foods that reminded him of the old country. He would get halvah, a sweet candy bar made from crushed sesame, pickled herring, and his favorite delicacy, salmon roe, which he called caviar. The final stop was the bakery, where they would buy the heavy rye bread that you could never get in a grocery store. He refused to eat white bread. He called it "cotton bread." Of course, they bought rugalach. Rugalach was a type of cookie/pastry. It was rolled up like a crescent and made with sugar, cinnamon, and I do not know what else.

When we came home, I sat with my father to enjoy the repast. He might have a shot of slivovitz or grain alcohol. I was told that a shot of either of the two, once a week, would keep you healthy. That is what his father drank. I could not eat the whitefish with the head on it. I did relish the lox, pickled herring, and thick slices of rye bread with butter and covered in salmon roe. Each salmon egg popped in my mouth. I loved the small explosion of salty oil unlike no other food. Dad and Mom would talk about their childhood. It was a time before the war. They were proud to be Polish and Jewish. They talked about school and being children. As they savored the delicacies, they were not just enjoying food. The food brought back the good memories, memories of their mothers' kitchens and their fathers' wisdom. It brought back their memories of a free Poland where they did not experience overt anti-Semitism. My father was playing with his friends and riding in the cart with his father. My mother was in the arms of her grandmother and waiting for her uncle David to come and share his stories.

It was a break in time. It was a respite. It was Melville's tranquil, lovely, azure waters beneath which lurked the monsters. Secretly the whale was leading them out to sea to a place where you could not be sure who was the angel and who was the devil, any more than Ahab's first mate could.

My mother cooked the chicken soup. She cooked the carp, tasting it regularly, even though it was still raw, and adding the ingredients as needed. She had no idea about written recipes. She went purely by taste. At dinner I would not eat the gefilte fish because it looked gross. I did not like the soup. I much preferred Campbell's Chicken Soup. I was only ten years old. My father told me that I had no idea of what good food is. I could hear the growing impatience in his voice. We had better finish what was on our plates. He could not stand to see food thrown in the trash. If there was mold or rot, you cut it away and ate the good part. I was astonished to find children at school with the crust cut off the bread. I would not dream of asking my mother to waste bread that way. Finally, the rugalach was brought out. I preferred Oreos or chocolate chip cookies. Soon the angry lecture came out. It turns out I was spoiled, he said. "You should know what it is like to starve for a few days." He wasn't talking about the children in Africa or Asia. He was reliving his own starvation. To waste the good food that my mother put on the table was among the great betrayals, and a sin.

It was time to be careful. One disrespectful answer, and my jaw would be numb from a slap before I knew it was coming. At some point, I explained that this was the food he was used to. I had become used to American food. I ate canned chicken soup at home for lunch and something similar every day at the school cafeteria. My taste buds were simply not trained the way his were. I had already read the biography of Clarence Darrow, a legendary trial lawyer. It was at that point that my father should have understood I should be headed for law school. With a reasonable argument he would usually back off, so I learned to reason well. I got used to thinking up arguments for common problems with my father. I had a ready portfolio. I got used to asking for proof that I had committed the act I was accused of. After all, he was the man who could reason with an armed robber or think up a scheme like breaking his own nose to avoid going to prison. He ought to be able to outwit his son.

As I grew, I came to appreciate my mother's soup and her gefilte fish to a point where I still consider it so perfect that I can hardly bear eating anyone else's homemade gefilte fish or soup, let alone the ready-made stuff. Every time I do, I say to myself that it simply is not my mother's. I miss her soup. I miss the pierogi. I would come home from college on break and drive back with two coolers in the back of my VW Beetle. One had frozen pierogi; the other had soup, steaks, and a homemade apple pie. Her apple pie was not gooey. She used tart green apples and put all the sugar on the crust. It is the only apple pie I would ever like. She loved the stories of me feeding it to my roommate, Hoppy Kercheval. She loved the way I would mimic those mountain accents and tell her over and over about how my guests would say, "Oh, boy. More of Miz Bruner's Pie Rogies."

For the rest of my father's life, under the tranquil azure waters of family gatherings, homemade food, teaching me watchmaking, and reminiscing about the good things in life, Ahab and the whale were still tangling with each other. Sometimes he was the whale, and sometimes he was Ahab. It all depended on the circumstances.

Fifteen

THE PHOENIX: MATES BRUNER

For there is no folly of the beast of the earth
which is not infinitely outdone by the madness of men
—HERMAN MELVILLE, *MOBY-DICK*

When I turned eighty, my children had a surprise party for me at the Union League in Philadelphia. It was a very happy moment. Every birthday was a gift. Eighty was a special milestone. Joe, Sam, and Halina gave speeches. Sam read the poem, "Do Not Go Gentle into That Good Night" by Dylan Thomas. When Sam was sad, I sometimes told him that he should not let the light go out. I did not let the light go out. I did not go gentle into that good night. I raged for most of my life. It was something I had learned in the war, and I never learned to stop.

The war had finally ended, and now I rode a bicycle over six hundred kilometers across the German landscape to Prague. Schindler had moved his factory there, and I wanted to find Halina. There was hunger everywhere. The cities had been bombed. I rode through Hanover. The city center was gone. Over six thousand civilians died in the bombings. Somehow it seemed like they were getting off easy. There was a labor camp nearby, where mostly Poles were interred.

There had been ten thousand prisoners there. At the end of the war, there were only two hundred left. Some cities had been spared, but it looked like most cities were destroyed as long as they were important industrial or fuel refining cities, rail centers, or large population centers.

I rode through Brunswick, Magdeburg, Leipzig, and right down through Dresden. Everything was in ashes, and the roads were clogged with refugees. In Dresden and Hamburg, the intensity of the fire was so great that a self-feeding ball of fire rose from the ground. It was so hot the asphalt was on fire. While unanticipated by the Allies, the fire rose into a tornado funnel, taking the air and even people with it. Everyone and everything that was pulled in was evaporated by fire. Hiroshima could not have been worse. Just as the clouds of ashes rose over the extermination camps, now Germany was covered in ashes of defeat and the burned corpses of their own population.

During the war, I had no time to ponder. I was completely focused on survival. This ride would take almost three months, so I had time to think for the first time in almost five and a half years. All I knew was that such a hatred arose in the Nazis that they would end up bringing destruction to their people and to the other peoples of Europe. I watched as the Ukrainians and Lithuanians joined the Germans, not so much to fight their war but rather in their murder of civilians. The Russians were almost as bad as they rolled through Eastern Europe, raping and pillaging. They murdered their prisoners, raped and murdered women and girls, and took what little valuables the Nazis had left. In the camps, the prisoners turned on one another for a crumb of bread. The kapos took advantage of the weakest.

This whole war had shown me the worst in humanity. It didn't matter what religion or nationality you were. It didn't matter if you were in a camp or on a battlefield. It didn't matter what side you were on. When it was a matter of personal or national survival, everyone forgot his humanity. It seemed that anyone, and almost everyone, could become an animal if the conditions were right.

There were acts of bravery and great acts of kindness, but they were far too few to make a difference to most of us. I rode through this barren, postapocalyptic landscape full of cinders, rubble, and a people who had become almost as pitiful as the people their government had oppressed. Still, except for acts of retribution and atrocities by Soviet soldiers, the Germans were being treated a whole lot better than they had treated others, and they darn well knew it. I had a Star of David flag on my bike. All I had to do was stop where I saw Allied refugee camps or groups of soldiers, and I had food and shelter. Meanwhile, the German people were turned into beggars.

I lived in the farmer's barn for seven weeks. The village was called Seppensen. Every day I felt a little stronger. I had hope that my family was alive. The German armies were surrendering, but the fighting went on. The fighting stopped in early May, but the official surrender of the German government did not occur until the end of May. I did not have to sleep under the haystack anymore, but the farmer was afraid for me (and maybe himself), so he suggested I stay awhile. Finally, in June, he marched me into town and presented me to the bürgermeister. The townsfolk treated me very kindly, and the farmer was also congratulated for his courage. Earlier in the war, they would have thrown stones at me. Now, they were throwing their last bits of bread.

I was finally free, and the feeling of freedom was intoxicating. I had risen like the phoenix from the ashes of the camps. It was Germany that was now in ashes, literally and metaphorically. We will forever look back and debate whether Germany paid enough of a price in blood and destruction, along with living in a divided nation and the fear of invasion for over fifty years.

Unlike Japan or East Germany, the West Germans admitted their crimes and paid reparations. By 1950 more than twelve million Germans had been expelled from East European lands. Some had moved in during the war, but most had lived there for many generations. The Allies wanted to create, as much as possible, ethnically homogeneous states. Like others, most of these people lost their ancestral homes and fled with what they could carry. Had it been any other nationality, the world would have known, but it was very hard to feel sorry for the Germans, even when you knew there were innocent people involved.

Had their fate been left to the Russians, it would have gone much harder for them. As far as this war was concerned, the term "innocent civilian" encompassed more people, more hardship, and more misery than the human mind could possibly comprehend. Stalin was right. A number this large can only be a statistic. Who cared about twelve million displaced German civilians when almost six million innocent Jewish civilians, two million innocent Polish civilians, eighteen million innocent Russian civilians, and millions more innocent civilians from other nations were murdered? How many millions of young men perished on the battlefield or in prison camps? Perhaps the most incalculable cost to the Germans would be the explanation they would have to give to their children and grandchildren for what happened. How many had to lie so their offspring would not think of them as monsters?

The score could never be even. There was no way to compute the cost. Too many Nazis got away or were not punished because the Western Allies now feared the Soviet Union too much, and the fall of China in 1948 would only make it worse. Poland would have to live in slavery again. The Allies betrayed them in 1939, and they were being betrayed again. America had all the power. As much as we saw Roosevelt, Truman, and Eisenhower as the great saviors, their almost childish naïveté regarding Stalin was astonishing. Churchill knew what would happen. General George Patton, notwithstanding his desire to use German troops, had it right.

The Soviet victory was a Pyrrhic victory. The Americans could have marched over them. They could have driven them back to their borders. They were the only atomic power. Stalin might even have fallen. The Americans were at their military zenith, but they walked away and left Eastern Europe to its fate. How could anyone deal with Stalin, a monster as great as Hitler, after what had happened? What kind of joke was Nuremberg when Russians passed judgment on Germans and had them put to death for "breaking the peace"? Had they forgotten the Molotov-Ribbentrop pact? Were they so blind they could not see the calculated imprisonment and murder of German and Eastern European leaders who wanted to bring democracy and freedom to their countries?

Did they not know about the vengeance Stalin was bringing onto the heads of the Ukrainian and Lithuanian people? It is not that I felt much more sympathy for them than for the Germans, but like the Germans, so many of them were innocent civilians caught up in the war and just trying to survive under whatever regime controlled them.

Food was scarce, but my entire thought process was no longer focused on food or survival. I no longer wished that I were a horse or a cow. I was not a slave, a prisoner, or a pitiful wretched Jew. I was a free man. I could go where I pleased and say what I wanted to.

On June 23, 1945, the bürgermeister presented me with a bicycle and a letter stating:

I attest the watchmaker Mates Brunengraber born 29.10.1920 in Krakau, that his family was murdered by the Nazis because they were Jewish. He could only save himself by jumping out of the train on the way to Belsen. He had been in a concentration camp for about three years. After living for seven weeks in a small village he now wishes to look for his sister who is about sixteen years of age. His sister was, like him, dragged away to a concentration camp near Prague. Please help Mr. B. to get to Prague. Give him general support including food and employment.

The Bürgermeister of Seppensen

Many people had no papers of any kind, and you just did not know what kind of mess you could end up in. This letter was very helpful as I moved among the Allied zones. I considered the Americans the kindest soldiers I have ever met. They lacked for nothing, and they gave away everything they could to the refugees. My opinion is not just the reflection of my own experiences but also that of any refugee I met. The Germans would do anything they could to surrender to the Americans. The Americans molested no one. They were from a faraway land. They had no ancient axe to grind. They did not come seeking revenge. They came to put things in order and hopefully leave. These people were different. While Ukrainians and Poles had fought over their version of Catholicism, while national and ethnic hatreds erupted because the war allowed them to, while Jews were hated because they were a convenient scapegoat, while the Roma were interned and Jehovah's witnesses ended up in camps, the Americans did not understand the reasons. They represented all of these groups and more.

You could not say what an American was other than they were dark, light, redheaded, black, every possible Christian denomination, and Jewish. They came from small towns in Texas and villages in Alaska. They were Japanese and American Indian. They were from New York and Billings, Montana. They understood they were Americans. We just didn't know exactly what that meant. We did not know how to define a nationality that had no national religion, race, ideology, or ethnicity. By Nazi standards, they were the most bastardized people on earth, but it was the badge of pride for the Americans. If the true measure of a people is that their actions speak louder than words, then the Americans were angels. They comforted us and seemed to be at their happiest when they were feeding and sheltering us. I don't know how they were in battle. Maybe they didn't have enough hate in them to be as fierce as other armies, but their equipment was top rate, they ruled the skies and the seas, and there was no end to it. Germany could not fight a war on two fronts. From Berlin to Moscow was less than twelve hundred miles, and the German supply lines could not keep up.

Goering said the Americans were only good at making razor blades. Yet the Americans could fight across two oceans, destroy their enemies, and supply their allies with food, armaments, and money. They destroyed the Japanese navy and built so many carriers that they filled the ocean skies with planes. When German soldiers looked out over the Atlantic on D-Day, they saw more ships than ocean. The Americans established air superiority immediately, and their huge bombers destroyed every target. Their tanks covered the plains. Everything was the finest, from their uniforms right down to their chewing gum, chocolates, and cigarettes. Every single soldier had, at a minimum, an M1 Garand rifle. They could fire faster and more accurately because they were semiautomatic. Their machine guns were .45 caliber and could slice a man in two. Their streets must have been paved in gold.

They exuded confidence, not in victory, but in their own abilities and sense of justice. Their engineers came not just to blow things up but also to rebuild. They were easygoing and willing to bend the rules if it was expedient and helpful to others. Without them, the aftermath of the war would have been a lot harder on the refugees. They were not afraid to hold even the dirtiest and smelliest among us. None of us ever seemed beneath them. Without them, there would be no freedom in Europe.

They did not invade until June 1944. Some people say the war had turned with the surrender at Stalingrad in February 1943. Certainly, by the end of the battle of Kursk that summer, the Germans were on the retreat and would not be able to mount another major offensive. The Soviet military horde moved inexorably forward. It is hard to know what would have happened to Continental Europe if the Allies had not invaded France, and no invasion was possible without the Americans.

Halina was not in Prague. "Whatever happens, when the war is over we will meet back in Krakow," I had said to Helen and Halina before we parted. To Halina, this was almost a bad joke. She did not share the confidence I had. I feared she would not make it, but it turns out she had more guts than I thought, and Schindler was her guardian angel. I asked around for information. I was told that the Russians had liberated the area, and the people from Schindler's factory were given transportation back to Krakow. The Russians did not molest them. From Prague, I left on my bike for Krakow. There were more refugees clogging the bombed-out roads and suspicious characters to watch out for. From the air, it must have just looked like a swarm of ants.

I came to Krakow almost three months after leaving Seppensen. I had traveled about eleven hundred kilometers. At least my legs were in good shape. Poor Halina, she had come to Krakow as quickly as she could. She was considering smuggling herself into Palestine with some people she met at the factory, but she decided she had to get to Krakow to find her family. She had been there three months, waiting and losing hope. She was now truly alone and feared that everyone else had died.

Our reunion was the happiest and most joyful single moment I had since the beginning of the war. Later, Helen would come along with an amazing story of courage and survival. Soon Daneck and Berta showed up. They did not want to live in Boryslaw anymore. They'd had enough of the Ukraine. At least now, I felt I had a family. We would support each other and see what came down the road.

Halina came to Plaszow only days before the Jews of the village of Slomnicki were rounded up and shipped away. We had heard about it in the camp. Halina, in a show of great courage, went to a high-ranking SS officer. She begged and pleaded with him to give her a pass to travel to Slomnicki. He could have beat or even killed her. Instead, he gave her the pass. When she told others she had the pass, they were shocked. They would never have even thought to ask. The officer was probably sorry for his act of weakness. Once again, a murderer showed an act of kindness. What did it really matter to him? In the end, we were all supposed to die anyway.

Halina found out that Laser was hiding in the basement of a Christian family, who took him in when my mother asked them because Helen had been tutoring their children. The neighbor was one of those brave Poles who were willing to show pity and put her own family's life at risk. Halina learned that it was Ukrainians, and not Germans, who came to round them up. Laser was in the basement and could see through a window that his parents were being taken away. He could see his father stabbed with a bayonet because he did not move fast enough. Laser started screaming and ran out of the house to his family. A guard shot him down. He was just a boy who wanted to help his family. He was no threat. We assumed my parents and Sabina went to Auschwitz but learned later they went to Belzec, which was also an extermination camp. We waited for them in Krakow, hoping against all odds that they would return to us, but that was not going to happen.

Daneck, as a returning hero, could have any apartment he wanted. As Krakow was spared any bombing, most of the city looked as it had before the war. I was looking at an apartment building near the center of town. I pointed it out to Daneck. I told him he could get an apartment a few floors up, and I could put a watchmaker's sign up. I didn't plan to do much watchmaking. We went up to the apartment. We knew that German civilians lived there and that they would be moved out eventually. A German woman lived in the apartment I wanted. Daneck came in his uniform. I had learned to speak German very well, after having been a guest of their government for so long. I told the woman that Daneck wanted her apartment. She could wait and be forced out, or she could take some money and leave. She did the smart thing and took the money. I put up a sign and started my first business.

People were hungry and willing to sell what few possessions they had. Word got around. I did not need much to start with. I started repairing watches and made some money. I bought gold and sold it for currency. I exchanged currencies, making a profit with every transaction. I bought British pounds and exchanged them for dollars. Rubles, kopecks, francs, deutschmark, gold, silver, watches, pens…anything of value that was portable, I traded. It seemed as though people were so stunned by the war, they were still just surviving instead of thriving.

It was a great business for a while, but the government was slowly becoming communist. Opposition politicians were being arrested. The government banned trading in foreign currencies. I kept doing business, but the writing was on the wall. The police sent in an undercover detective one day to trade currencies. At the close of business, I hid everything in a carefully crafted false bottom dresser. In the middle of the night, the police came smashing against my door with the butts of their rifles. They arrested me and took me to the police station. As they questioned me, they were also tearing up my apartment, but they never found what they were looking for. They had to let me go. I had lived through Hitler, and I was not going to hang around Poland so I could be one of Stalin's victims. Berta, Daneck, Halina, Helen, and I agreed it was time to go to Palestine.

Sixteen

THE PALESTINE QUESTION

A land without a people for a people without a land
—FAMOUS ZIONIST SLOGAN

I sat in a restaurant with an Egyptian friend, or at least someone who I thought was a friend. I have traveled to Israel six times and to Egypt before it recognized Israel, along with many other Muslim countries. In most cases, the Muslims I spoke to were willing to accept moderate Israeli viewpoints, provided I was willing to believe and accept their views of the need for a Palestinian state in order to obtain peace in the region. The Middle East has changed, and, in many ways, the positions on all sides are harder and far less conciliatory.

Had this been twenty years earlier, this Egyptian man and I would probably have found a way to see eye to eye. However, in his old age, he had decided to become a devout Muslim. It was Ramadan. It was seven thirty in the evening, and he still had not had any food or water. It wasn't my desire to discuss Middle East politics. If anything, I talked mostly of my trip to Egypt and how nice everyone had been to me. We talked about our families. I related a summary of my father's background and said how one could understand his desire to move to Israel and the decision of diaspora Jews to support it.

"I completely reject this logic as a justification for Israel," he said quite firmly as he slapped his hand on the table.

"I did not say that it was a valid justification; I was expressing the feelings and emotions of my father and others like him," I replied. "You do not have to agree with people's opinions, but if you cannot begin to understand their motivations, then you can never have peace. Understanding the other side's viewpoint," I told him, "without agreeing with them is the basis for mediation and compromise."

This little episode speaks a great deal to the current situation. Everyone wants to blame someone, and there seems to be a wide gap in the area of compromise. Over time, I have concluded that most of the fault lies with the British. Prior to World War I, the Turks ruled this land. The region was known as Greater Syria. The northeastern part was called Mesopotamia. The western portion was referred to as Syria, with a Christian minority congregated in an area known as the Lebanon. The Arabian Peninsula was known as Arabia and ruled by the Saud family. The west coast strip along the Red Sea of the Arabian Peninsula, including Mecca and Medina, was known as the Hejaz under the rule of the Hashemites. Gaza was ruled by Egypt. The remaining land, then referred to as Palestine, was an area that today includes Jordan, the Golan Heights of Syria, southern Lebanon, and all the area that is today known as Israel and the West Bank. Had you asked an Arab farmer or a Jewish farmer in 1910 in the area that today is Israel or the West Bank, you might get the same answer, "I live in the area of Palestine, part of Greater Syria in the Ottoman Empire." For the most part, there were no strong independence movements. The Muslims and other minorities were content to be ruled by the Turks, who left them alone, provided they obeyed their laws and paid their taxes to the governors, who kicked some of the money upstairs to the sultan.

A minority of Jews had lived in the area. Young, idealistic Zionist pioneers had been coming to the area since the mid-to-late-nineteenth century. This number started to increase at the turn of the century with the revival of pogroms in Poland and Russia, culminating in the Kishinev massacre. A riot, based on the blood libel of two Christian children who had died, started on Easter Sunday, 1903, and went on for three days. About forty-nine Jews were killed, almost six hundred injured, and seven hundred homes destroyed. Many businesses were burned and looted. France was also in turmoil over the Dreyfus Affair that started in 1894 and was not resolved until 1906. What is important to note about all of this is that the Zionists who came to Palestine bought land from the Arabs, who were happy to sell it to them. There was plenty of land; the Jews were settling in areas where there was no, or very little, local population. Much of it was desert, uncultivated, or swamp. Even the city of Tel Aviv, where a large portion of the Israeli population lives today, was founded on barren sand dunes north of Jaffa. They were a skilled and educated work force; they increased the wealth of the region and brought jobs for everyone. They planted trees and reforested the land that had been laid barren by the Turks, who had used the wood to build their railroads.

Many people believe the Zionists only wanted a modern nation-state. That is not true. While some did—and most came to believe, between the wars, that this was the only viable option as Arab hostility increased— the goal was a national homeland for the Jews. This could just as easily have been an autonomous region under the Turks, who were quite content with the increased tax revenues. There was also no need to agitate against the Turks, as their reprisals could be brutal. Under the treaty of Brest-Litovsk, Russian Armenia was handed over to the Turks. The Armenians were not happy with the arrangement, and the Turks killed between one and one and a half million of them during and after the war.

There was a split among the Zionists. Some were pro-British, and others were status quo. The status quo group did not want to be part of a geopolitical struggle. They just wanted to create a land where Jews could live in peace and live free from persecution. There seemed to be plenty of land. Even at the end of World War I, there were Palestinian leaders willing to accept a multinational land ruled under a British mandate. Whether it was the Turks or the British made little difference. Those who sided with the British, such as Chaim Weizmann, were betrayed in the end by Great Britain.

When World War I started, the Ottomans allied themselves with the Germans. There were several British moves that may have pushed them toward the Germans. Also, the Turks believed it was possible the British might lose the war, and the Turks could move into Egypt, or at least take the Suez Canal. The British, not content with defending the canal zone where they easily beat back the Turks, declared war on Turkey, with the intent of dismantling the empire along with Anatolia itself. In order to have the necessary troops, they needed permission from the French to withdraw troops from France, which was fighting a war of national survival. The Sykes-Picot secret agreement was formed whereby the British would take the area from the Turks, and the French would get a piece of the action when the war was over.

The English invaded Palestine and moved northward toward Damascus. Mr. T. E. Lawrence was sent to Arabia to organize the Bedouins. They would fight the Turks in Arabia, thus securing the British right flank, with the British left flank protected by the sea. In time, the French were handed the country now known as Syria and a new Christian majority country known as Lebanon. The land across the Jordan River was given to the Hashemite prince, Abdullah, for his help in fighting the Turks. British officers trained his army. The British government gave away the area that became Transjordan, the Golan Heights to Syria, and Southern Lebanon to the new Christian majority Lebanese state, leaving only about 25 percent of the land that should have been Palestine.

Though the war had ended in 1918, the final resolution of all claims would not occur until 1922. The League of Nations, which granted the British Mandate of Palestine, did not differentiate Transjordan (now Jordan) with the area west of the Jordan River that is today Israel and the West Bank. Churchill convened the Cairo Conference in March

1921 and made clear his intention that the area east of the Jordan River would be a Palestinian homeland under the rule of Abdullah, and the area west of the Jordan would become the Jewish homeland, which, like Egypt, would have partial independence, with Britain controlling foreign policy and having unrestricted troop movement. By doing so, and granting kingdoms to the Hashemites who fought against the Turks, Britain could argue it had made good on its wartime promises. Jews were precluded from settling east of the Jordan River. This cut them off from the Upper Jordan, Litani, and Yarmuk Rivers and the rich plains east of Lake Tiberius that had been the most favorable area for large-scale Jewish settlement.

Both Jewish and Palestinian leaders now became worried about sharing land that was only 25 percent of their perception of what Palestine was. Zionists, both convincingly and realistically, believed that, with a modern economy based on cutting-edge agricultural techniques and manufacturing technology, along with the continued import of some of the brightest scientific minds from Europe, the land would become wealthy and easily support a population more than ten times the 1920 population of six hundred thousand Jews. The Palestinian leaders did not understand the concept of dynamics. Their view was clearly static; there was a limited amount of land and water, and although things were fine for now, if there were to be the large-scale immigration the Zionists hoped for, the Arabs would be squeezed out. Moreover, even if what the Zionists and the British leaders were saying was true, the Palestinian Arab leaders were not interested in change, modernization, or living any differently than they had before the war. They were content under the Turks, and if they had to have rulers, they preferred that they be Muslim.

Whereas Churchill, Lord Balfour, and Lloyd George were all Christian restorationists (an Evangelical wing of the Anglican church that supported the return of the Jews to Palestine, the rebuilding of the Temple, the Jews' conversion to Christianity, and the birth of the messianic age), the British bureaucrats settling into the administration of the territories were Arabists. The Arabs had lived there for ages, and their wishes were to be respected. The bureaucrats wanted safety and comfort and did not want riots. The Arabs were the majority, and the best way to have a peaceful, comfortable administration of the area was to listen to them.

Seventeen

WALDENBURG: MATES BRUNER

By the rivers of Babylon, there we sat down,
yea, we wept, when we remembered Zion.
Upon the willows in the midst thereof we hanged up our harps.
For there they that led us captive asked of us
words of song, and our tormentors asked of us
mirth: "Sing us one of the songs of Zion."
How shall we sing the Lord's song in a foreign land?

If I forget thee, O Jerusalem, let my right
hand forget her cunning.
Let my tongue cleave to the roof of my
mouth, if I remember thee not;
if I set not Jerusalem above my chiefest joy.

—PSALM 137:1–6

I saw her playing volleyball, folk dancing, and talking to other men. She was the center of attention. She was only seventeen. She was the healthiest-looking refugee I knew. Her skin was perfect. Her figure was a classic, shapely 1940s figure. She exuded life and energy. Her name was

Wanda Drapacz. I had feelings that I had not felt since before the war. I had to talk to her. I had to have her. She was the first person I met who was not somatized or so traumatized by what had gone on that she lost her vivacity and love of life.

Since the end of the war I had not looked upon women with desire. I was dead inside. In my mind's eye, I still saw the emaciated bodies, dead bodies, live bodies, and those in between. That is all I could see when I looked at a woman. There was no desire in me for any kind of relationship. The only thing that had occupied my mind for so long was my survival and that of my sisters. Wanda was different. She was a beam of precious light that cut through all these thoughts and made me think about the future. Her energy became my energy. I was destined to be with her.

It was March of 1946. I had come to Waldenburg with Helen, Halina, Daneck, and Berta. Waldenburg was in Poland, very close to the Czech border. Just as before the war, Jews could get exit visas, but not entry visas to other countries. The Zionists were very actively trying to smuggle Jews out of Poland and, hopefully, to Palestine. They organized a variety of activities for refugees. That is how I came to meet Wanda. There were several Zionist factions in Waldenburg organizing an underground railway.

The Jews wanted to get to Palestine, but the British had an embargo, and there was no legal way to proceed. There were several routes, all of them dangerous. The easiest way was by train to Czechoslovakia, but Polish partisans often attacked them. The partisans still had their guns, and they attacked Jewish refugees, robbing them and then killing them. They blamed the Jews for the war, and they seemed intent on finishing the job the Nazis had started. Another route was by foot over the mountains using local Poles as guides; some were trustworthy, many were not. Helen met a man named Jacob Wischnia. He was organizing and leading groups of Jews across the mountains.

Jacob had spent the war fighting with the Polish brigades under the Russians as an infantryman. This was possibly the worst fighting that anyone saw. He was fearless and more than willing to risk his life for others.

He fought on the battlefield, and he fought in house-to-house combat. Jacob, like the others he fought with and against, had only one concern: to kill as many of the enemy as possible. "Kill the German." It was the battle cry of every Russian soldier. At the same time, for as long as I knew him, he was a kind, gentle man. He and Helen fell in love. They tried to get to Palestine right after the war. Unfortunately, like so many others, they were unable to get out of Europe at the time.

As I got to know Wanda better, I was enchanted with her. I could hardly keep my eyes off her. She wasn't interested much in books or discussing ideas. I gave her books to read so that we would have more to discuss. She tried, but she got bored. It was a disappointment to me, but I believed in time she would want more stimulation. I needed a soul mate and hoped she would be the one. I was twenty-five now. She looked up to me. We went on hikes and picnics in the hills and attended the gatherings arranged by the Zionist organizations. I was beginning to see some beauty in the world.

I wanted to get out of Poland. The government wanted us to stay. We were told things would be different under a socialist government. Everyone would be equal. I had heard that before in my youth. I had utterly no desire to live in a socialist country; and any fool could see the Russians were pulling the puppet strings, and it was only a matter of time until it was communist. People like me with business aspirations would be crushed. Then there were the pogroms. There were a number of incidents, some near Waldenburg, where Polish citizens accused Jews of blood libel. A Polish child was found dead near the Hashomer Kibbutz, and many Poles blamed the Jews. The Jewish owner of a store chased a Polish woman who stole shoes from him. She ran down the street, screaming that Jews were after her. A mob started to form, but the police broke it up before there was trouble. There were other incidents, but so far, the police had intervened and kept the situation calm.

There were still fascist bandits in the forest committing crimes. Bandits at Tiraspol, the first stop after leaving the Russian frontier, attacked a train carrying repatriated Jews from the Soviet Union to Poland. There were more incidents. The Jewish Telegraph Agency was our main source of news. Other news sources did not carry this kind of information. Even Cardinal Sapieha of Krakow made a statement that the reason for the recent pogroms against the Jews in Poland was due to Jews holding so many government positions. Once again, the church was busy whitewashing what had happened and somehow reaching for an excuse. At least he admitted there had been violence. Many said the Jews were just creating propaganda. Finally, there was the pogrom in Kielce on July 4, 1946.

Three days earlier, a nine-year-old Polish boy was reported missing. It turns out he had gone to visit relatives in another town. When he came home, he said an old man who did not speak Polish had kidnapped him. The family believed it was a Jew or a Gypsy. As the father walked with the boy to the police station, they passed a building where about 150 Jewish refugee families were living. The father asked his son if this was where he was taken. The boy said yes and pointed to a young man standing outside, saying he was the kidnapper. The boy claimed he had been held in the basement of the house.

The fact that the house had no basement, or that the man he was pointing to was young, made little difference. Police, military, and civilians converged on the house. The Jews living there had been allowed by the government to keep guns for their self-protection. The police came in and ordered them to give up their guns and valuables. Fighting broke out. A mob surrounded the property. The police shot randomly in the house and looted the property. Soldiers came and helped some of the Jews out of the building. The mob killed many of them. Wounded Jews were transported to the hospital. Soldiers beat and robbed them during the transport. Civilians marched to the hospital and demanded that the wounded Jews be brought out. The hospital staff refused and protected them.

Mobs in other parts of Kielce attacked Jewish homes. In one case, a Jewish woman and her baby were dragged from their house and killed.

Forty-two Jews died that day, and at least forty were injured. Trains passing through Kielce were stopped, and Jewish passengers were beaten. This went on for several months and cost the lives of at least thirty additional Jews. The dead and wounded were former soldiers who had fought for Poland's freedom along with concentration-camp survivors. Two Poles who tried to help Jews were also killed. In the following months, between seventy-five thousand and ninety thousand Jews left Poland and headed for freedom, or at least to displaced-person camps in the American Zone.

From the end of the war in May of 1945 to the end of the summer of 1946, as many as 150,000 Jews left Poland. This mass underground migration through Czechoslovakia, Hungary, and the Russian-occupied zone of Germany and Austria to the American Zone in Austria, Germany, and Italy would fill the displaced-person camps and cause tremendous pressure for the Allies. British soldiers from the Jewish brigade helped, and American commanders often turned a benign blind eye to the refugees coming into their jurisdiction. Once again, the Americans were helping us. They could have, and were supposed to, turn us away, but they didn't. Their sense of humanity would not allow it.

Why did this madness continue? What is it about human beings that so many must find differences so great they are willing to murder one another? It doesn't seem to matter whether it is race, religion, political beliefs, class, or nationality. I thought people would have learned something from this war. It is bad enough to forget what happened, but to forget, you must first remember. To remember something, there had to be an end. Here, there was no end. It was not time to remember, because there was no end to the horror.

I am sure that if we put one hundred people on an island who were all the same, in short order they would find a way to separate into groups, each feeling superior to the other. It is human nature. I did not have much schooling, but I surely was an educated man when it came to human behavior and mob mentality. I did not need Darwin to tell me that man ascended from animals. In many ways, based on what I experienced, man had descended from animals. Animals kill for food. They fight for other reasons, but not simply to kill one another.

I know there is good in the world, but it is sometimes a problem for me to see it, for what I have seen does not bode well for humanity. The only real good I ever saw was family helping family. The closest I have been to pure altruism was my experience with the Red Cross, American soldiers, and American civilians. There were brave, kind people in Russia, Germany, Poland, and even the Ukraine, but never did I see the quantity of courage and kindness as I saw in the Americans.

The Jews were finished with Poland. Only a few remained behind. Poland had made sure they were finished with the Jews. They hated the Germans and the Russians, but it seemed they hated the Jews even more. Poland was soaked in Jewish blood and ashes, and it seemed as though the Poles were happy about it.

Eighteen

Exodus: Wanda Bruner

We left at dark and rode all night through the Russian Zone. Every time the truck slowed down or stopped, our hearts jumped. By morning, we were in the American Zone of West Berlin. Mates made the arrangements for us. It was illegal and dangerous. We had to smuggle ourselves through the Russian Zone of Germany. To do so legally required a great deal of documentation and various permission papers. The Russians were looking for spies, ex-Nazis, and deserters. There were Polish smugglers who drove small trucks with only a few people in the back. We could not be sure they were trustworthy, but we took the chance anyway. It turns out they were good at what they did.

Mates was handsome and slender, with thick, wavy brown hair like my own. He seemed very smart, and, unlike a lot of survivors, he was full of ideas and already had money in his pocket. He was older and more sophisticated. What did I know? I was only seventeen. He thought I was an unblemished flower, just right for the picking. I had never had a man interested in me before. I had no time. I was always busy working and helping the family to survive. Now I had some time for myself.

My mother did not like him. She said he was too bossy, but then my mother generally wore the pants in the family. She was always the bread-winner. She always made more than my father, but I wasn't like her. I had not had time to be a teenager. My teenage years were lost to the war.

144

I wanted someone who would help support me while I had children of my own. Children whose youth would not be lost just trying to survive. Marrying Mates was my chance to break away.

Mates and I both wanted to go to Palestine. I was always ready for a scrap, and I had no qualms about picking up a gun if I needed to. I had wanted to be a soldier before and during the war. Outside of Yoshkar-Ola was a military training camp. Whenever I could, I would climb atop the wall and watch the training. The recruits would line up at attention. The officer would walk up and down the line, glaring at the young men. He would suddenly jam his stick into the gut of one of them. They were being trained to be hard. That was war, and I was not afraid of it. I thought it was fun to watch, and I was sure I could be as tough as any of those recruits.

We could not all leave at once. We had to travel in small groups. Jacob and Helen got to Austria. Halina went with Berta and Daneck to Berlin after us. My sister Elsa met a man named Sam. They made it to Munich. My mother, my father, and my brothers Abram and Gerry got to Austria. Mates wanted me to go with him. I was willing, but while we were still in Poland, my mother said I was not going anywhere with a man unless I was married. We had only known each other for six weeks, but we decided we would get married and have an adventure together. It all seemed so exciting.

I know that people may think it was a short time to know each other, and they are right; but at the time, that is how many people got married. They hardly knew each other. The war made us like that. We got so used to the idea of living in the moment, because you just did not know what the next day would bring or even if you would be alive. Life moved very quickly. The last six years had been a whirlwind struggle. Getting married and moving away did not seem as odd as it sounds. It was a miracle that we were alive. It was a miracle that we were still human beings. It was a miracle we were not filled with hate, the way the Poles, the Russians, and the Ukrainians were. We did not have time for hate. We only wanted to move on with living.

When we got off the truck in Berlin, the Americans were wonderful to us, and the Red Cross was there with help. Mates had enough money that we did not need to stay at a displaced-person camp for very long. The camps were overflowing with refugees. It seemed that everyone wanted to be in the American Zone, and despite all those refugees along with the German civilians, the Americans were able to accommodate us all. The Allies were pressuring Britain to allow immigration to Palestine. The Congress in America was debating about lifting their quotas and allowing refugees to come in. Mates was given papers by the German administration that said he was a victim of the fascists, and this allowed him privileges that the Germans did not have. Mates and I were the kind of people who were not going to wait around and wonder what would happen to us. We made our own luck.

After we got to Berlin, we decided to have a honeymoon by taking a river cruise. It was lovely. I had not known anything so beautiful in my life. Up until now, I had been the center of his attention. I was number one in someone's life. I was with someone who was looking after me, and it felt so good. One day Mates was talking to some people. Mates always liked to talk politics with people. I got bored with the political talk, so I told him I would take a walk and go to our room and wait for him to come and take me to dinner. The hours passed. I went to look for him, and he was still engaged with other people. I finally opened my mouth in front of all those people, a mouth Mates had not heard before. We got into our first serious fight. It would not be the last, and it would get worse as we both began to feel the disappointment in our beautiful vision of marriage. I was no longer his center. He seemed to have time for others, but little for me. I was fast becoming an attachment. I was someone pretty and cheerful who had to be available and in a good mood when it suited him. It was an awful awakening, but what could I do? I wanted to go home to my mother, but my mother would not let me. People did not get divorced in those days. My mother had told me not to marry him. Now I had to live with it and try to make the best of it.

Berlin was rubble, but on the edges of the city, there were still buildings standing. Mates got an apartment. He had priority because of his papers. He wanted to open a jewelry store and watchmaking shop. Germany is not like the United States. To open a jewelry store, you had to have a master's certificate either from a watchmaking school or a jewelry repair school. With his background, he had no trouble getting a certificate from a watchmaking school in Berlin.

While in school, we started hunting for a store. He did not intend to immediately open a watchmaking shop. His time was too valuable. There was much more money to be made buying from the Germans. They were hungry and poor, and they had plenty of heirlooms and jewelry to sell. Once again, he had priority in his choice of locations. Business was booming. We bought jewelry, silver statues, silverware, watches, and clocks. We either scrapped the gold and silver or put it in the cases to resell. I knew nothing about the business, but I learned quickly. Vodka, sugar, or jewelry—it didn't matter. Buying low and selling high is all you had to know.

We paid the highest prices to German widows and old people. When a German man came in who was fair- skinned, stood straight, and had a military bearing, he got the worst deal possible. We felt no shame. We knew quickly from a little conversation whether someone was a Nazi—or worse, a member of the Gestapo or SS. We felt quite comfortable knowing they were suffering. They thought they were the masters of the world. Now they were just begging for money from Jews. We had no sympathy. We paid an awful price during the war, but now we were on top, and we believed this was only fair.

One day a tall, blond, blue-eyed man came in. He carried himself like an officer. Mates had a way of talking to the Germans, and he guessed quickly who did what during the war. We were both sure he had been in the SS. He had a gold signet ring that was scratched up so you could not make out any initials. The top was square, and there were cutout leaves on the side. Underneath there was a marking that we could not make out. Mates was very happy when he bought that ring. The leaves on the sides were oak leaf clusters, he told me. That meant it was a military ring. He recognized the marking. It was from one of the SS schools, and they used secret markings to identify their units or fraternities. The top was scratched up to obscure the SS identification. Mates had his initials carved into the top of the ring and put a diamond in it. He left the secret marking on the underside. He wore it with pride, almost to the end of his life, before he gave it to my grandson Marcus. To him, it was a constant reminder of how things ended up, with him becoming a success and the SS officer begging for scraps. To him, it was a symbol of justice.

Business was good. We had a steady income from selling scrap gold and silver, and we had enough jewelry, watches, and clocks to fill the store. Some Germans were doing well enough to buy, and the American soldiers were good customers, too. "Wealthy" was a relative word in those days. We had a nice apartment, a business, nice clothes, and a car. This was wealthy, considering the times. Things were getting better in Berlin. The Germans worked hard to rebuild. Shopping areas and theaters opened up. We got along well with the Germans. They wanted to pretend that nothing happened. We could not pretend that nothing happened, but we wanted to move forward. Berlin became a beautiful, modern city. Located in East Germany, it quickly became the showplace to contrast east and west.

The city was lively at night, and the Kurfürstendamm became the place to see and be seen. The Americans were everywhere. I liked them and began to wonder what America must be like. I had never seen a black man before, but here they were in uniform, walking around with the white soldiers. The soldiers were easygoing, friendly, and had money to spend. Some Germans did not like their lack of formality, especially the American children. English does not have a formal tense, so they tended not to use it when they spoke German. If an American child spoke to a German adult, he or she would use the informal greeting. Some Germans thought it was insulting. I thought it was refreshing.

I cannot recall an act of rudeness or meanness by the Americans, even though they were the victors. I could not tell what nationality an

American was. Their last names were English, German, French, Irish, Polish, Russian, Jewish, Italian, and last names I could not place at all. It did not seem like a nationality at all, but it was a nationality by virtue of the fact that they were not all the same. Who ever heard of a nationality defined by not having a nationality? There did not even seem to be an upper or lower class, at least in the army.

In 1948 two great events happened. In May, Israeli independence was declared. There would be a war, but Israel would survive. The shock of this reality would affect every Jew in the world. If a man had landed on the moon in 1948, it would have been less of a shock. We dreamed about it. We hoped for it. Many went to the land to build on it, but few believed it would become a reality. There is no doubt that the refugee problem was a great impetus, along with world sympathy. The Soviet Union was also glad to see a socialist country planted in the Middle East. The victory was bittersweet, knowing that this may not have happened had it not been for the war. Still, it was something to celebrate. The Jews had finally had a victory. They fought for this victory and changed the views of many regarding Jewish stereotypes.

In June 1948 the Soviets blocked all road and train access to Berlin from the west. The Berlin airlift began. No one believed enough supplies of food and fuel could come by air, but they did. The Americans, the British, the Canadians, the Australians, New Zealand, and South Africa all flew in supplies. The planes flew all day and all night. The bulk of it was American. The planes had to fly just above the rooftops in order to land at Tempelhof Airport. Many times, the Americans would drop candy out of the planes before landing, and the children would run out into the streets to collect it. With every act of kindness they showed, I loved the Americans more. Who else would bomb a city with candy?

My first child, Harry, had been born the previous October. I was happier than I had ever been. Mates and I were having our troubles. He was domineering, and he was very fixed in his ideas. Having a child together made things a lot better at home. Sometimes children have a way of bringing people together. It was the best time in our marriage. Our biggest worry came from the Berlin airlift. By the time it ended in 1949, Germany was formally divided and was now East Germany and West Germany. The Cold War had begun, and Berlin was ground zero if there was going to be fighting. We had enough of war. We had a child, and we had settled into peacetime living. We no longer thought of moving to Israel. I would still go, but Mates said he was tired of war and killing. He wanted to live and work in peace. I could not blame him, and deep inside, I guess I felt the same, especially now that I had a baby.

We had two options. We could emigrate to Sweden or America. Sweden was still Europe. It was peaceful and had stayed out of the war. America was a distant land, but we had a taste from living in the American Zone. We listened to American broadcasts on the radio and we heard the music. We loved Nat King Cole. We had not heard the voice of a black singer before. It was different from anything our ears had ever known. We even listened to early rock 'n' roll music. America was far away, but being far from Europe also meant safety. We would not know the language, but if the people were anything like the soldiers, we were sure we would be welcome. The Displaced Persons Act of 1948 would allow us to come to the United States without a sponsor.

Mates was unsure of what to do. His business had been doing well. He invented a rotating calendar that attached to a watchband. He started manufacturing it and put an ad in an international jewelry magazine. Orders came in from all over the world. It looked like he would be a very wealthy entrepreneur. He could not fill all the orders. He started manufacturing on a large scale with loans based on the orders. Within a year he was able to fill the orders, but the orders stopped coming. The base metal that was used was corroding, particularly in warmer climates when perspiration came in contact with it. We now had a large inventory and no orders. Mates would have to start over using different metals. He was nearly broke financially, but never broke spiritually. He would try again. He had no fear, but he knew it would be a hard road.

In January 1950 my son Joe was born. Later that year we received a letter from the Americans that the Displaced Persons Act was expiring and were given notice of the last date we could get on an American ship bound for New York. Mates had taken on a business partner. He sold his interest in the business to his partner. We decided without much debate to get on a ship with our babies in tow and make a new life in America.

It was a long ride on the ship. It took ten days to cross the ocean. There was plenty of room for the boys to run around. Harry was almost four, and Joe was almost two. I had never been on the open ocean before, with no land in sight, for so long. In Russia, the land stretched out forever. Now it was the ocean. Like the untold millions before us, we came into New York harbor. We passed the Statue of Liberty. Those who were born in America can never know the rush of emotions that ran through us as we viewed the statue. There are no words to describe it. As soon as we got off the boat, the Salvation Army was there to help. They had hot chocolate and cookies for the boys. Joe finished his cocoa and cookie and held up the cup, wanting more. They refilled it and gave him another cookie.

It was a good omen. This was America. The cup was full. Every year until his death, Mates sent a check to the Red Cross for all the help they gave in Europe. Every holiday season I made sure I put money in the Salvation Army bucket whenever I went by one, and I thought of that moment when they refilled Joe's cup.

Nineteen

THE ISRAELI

We are a generation of settlers,
and without the steel helmet or the gun barrel,
we shall not be able to plant a tree or build a house

—MOSHE DAYAN

In 1953 grenades were thrown through the open windows by two terrorists, followed by gunfire. Along the Mediterranean coast between Gaza and Tel Aviv, an Israeli couple was celebrating their wedding in their home, full of relatives and friends. The windows were open to allow the sea breeze in. The young couple was killed along with others, and many were wounded.

Gerald Drapacz, the youngest commissioned officer in the Israeli army, was assigned to lead the unit that would hunt them down. They tracked them down quickly. Gerald yelled in Arabic. They did not put up their hands. Gerald aimed his rifle, gave an order to fire, and killed one. Shots rang out from the soldiers around him, and the second fell to the ground. He approached the bodies. His orders were to capture them if at all possible. He had failed in that regard. In his own mind, he thought it was better this way. He was glad they did not surrender. They would not have to waste time on interrogations or paperwork. He already knew where they were from and what their objectives were. Their goals were not his goals. Their beliefs about the future of this land were not his beliefs. They were irreconcilable. They could not be settled by debate. They could only kill one another until they became so tired and weary of killing that they would finally find common ground, but this was not that time. Only the gun could settle the matter.

He was satisfied he had done his job. He felt nothing for them. Had these killers gone farther up the coast, they could just have easily thrown their grenades into his parents' house. Gerald and his team were army men, not policemen. Their job was to move fast and do their job quickly. The Israelis embraced the German philosophy of the blitz. They had to. They were few in number and could not withstand prolonged battles. Their weapon of choice was the Uzi assault rifle that had been invented for such a purpose. Based on a Czechoslovakian design, it was a simple 9-mm, machine-stamped, blowback weapon, designed for the soldier to run forward, yelling and firing on full auto, causing the enemy to be shocked and unprepared for the assault.

When I was a child, there was always a picture of Uncle Gerry around. In the family album was the picture of Gerry in his Israeli army uniform and beret. My mother and her family were extremely proud of him. He was the embodiment of their Zionist dreams. The rest of the family had become tired and weary from the war. They were already too old and worn down from the hellish fires they had gone through. Gerry was young, too young for his idealism and enthusiasm to have been crushed.

He was the youngest child in my mother's family. My grandparents came to Israel shortly after the war of independence in late 1948 or early 1949. My mother was married, as was her sister, Elsa. My uncles, Abram and Gerry, who were only teenagers, had to support my grandparents in their new country. My grandfather, Marcus, was a tailor, but he was old and suffered from Parkinson's disease. He only had sporadic work. My grandmother, Rachael, who could neither read nor write, had been the main breadwinner. She was the one who kept the family together and alive during the war years in Russia. Now she was weak and frail.

In Israel, there was a certain tension between some of the new arrivals and some of the Israelis who either came as children or were "Sabras" (native-born). The fault lies with both sides, and in many ways, it was inevitable. The native Israelis and those who had come before the Shoah had become used to fighting. They fought the British and the Arabs. They taught the desert to bloom; drained the swamps; and built cities, towns, schools, and hospitals. In short, they created a country from their sweat and blood. What the final borders would look like, whether there would ever be peace with the Arab community, was up in the air. Their attitude was simple. They were not going to leave. They were going to stay. They were going to fight if necessary or die in the process.

They were so focused on making a home in a land where they were no longer welcome that they had a difficult time empathizing or understanding the attitudes of the Europeans who allowed themselves to be slaughtered without a fight. They welcomed the fighters from the British Army, the Polish soldiers fighting in exile, and those who fought as partisans. The rest were sheep, and Israel needed fighters.

Of course, this was not fair. People were trying to survive as best they could. They tried to protect their families, and considering that other groups and nationalities also died by the millions, you could not call these people cowards. Those who could fight in armies did. Those who could join the partisans did. Most partisans in Eastern Europe, excluding communists such as Tito and the Russians, either did not allow the Jews to join or murdered them. The Israelis were simply from a different neighborhood and could not comprehend the magnitude of the problem anymore than the rest of the world could, when the number of dead was estimated at almost fifty million.

The common language of the European Jews was Yiddish. In Israel, they spoke Modern Hebrew and had a disdain for the language of the ghetto. This made training more difficult if Israeli officers did not speak

Yiddish. The survivors were physically weak and had no military training. Getting the Europeans trained quickly was impossible.

In the battle of Latrun, during the war of independence, 139 Shoah survivors, undernourished and sickly, without a common language, had a few days' training and were thrown into battle. Their assault up a hill was to start in the morning. Instead, it did not start until the afternoon under the burning sun. There were no provisions for bringing up water. They fought British-trained Jordanian legionnaires, who were behind a walled fortress. When it was over, half of them were dead, as many from heat exhaustion as from bullets. There is not one sign or marker indicating their heroism and willingness to die for their new country.

Many survivors came to Israel, as there was no place else to go. They would have gone to America if they could, so they were unhappy in Israel. The 1950s was a difficult time. Israel had few resources to help all the newcomers, and unemployment was high. After independence, the world forgot about Israel. The survivors, who still suffered from the mental anguish of the Shoah, were now in a land surrounded by tens of millions of Arabs who were screaming for Jewish blood.

Uncle Abram came to Israel not knowing Hebrew. He learned, of course, but most of his friends were also from Europe. He, like so many others, wanted to leave the hardship and come to America. He did in 1954, leaving only Gerry to support the family. Gerry's situation was different from Abram's. While in the displaced persons camps in Europe, Gerry went to classes to learn Hebrew. Gerry was very bright and would eventually earn his doctorate in economics and become a professor at MIT. When he arrived in Israel, he was only thirteen. As he spoke Hebrew, almost all of his friends were Sabras, and he integrated very quickly. He joined the GADNA, an Israeli youth organization where they taught patriotism and readied the men and women for their military service. Like his friends, he ached for the day when he could go into the army. It was not like the United States. There was no war beyond the seas. The Arab propaganda talked of driving the Jews into the sea. To be in the army was not just a question of serving your country. You were fighting for survival. When you were in the army, you were protecting your family and home from annihilation.

There were no public high schools at the time. All high schools were private, and Gerry did not have the money. He was able to get a job as a clerk at the Israel Electric Company. He returned to the company after the military services and rose to the rank of assistant production/operations manager at the young age of twenty-four years old. As a teenager, it was reasonable pay for the time—enough to pay the rent and grocery bills for him and his parents. Just as important, it would pay 80 percent of the tuition to a private high school, and Gerry loved learning. He also knew that opportunities would be limited without higher education. Gerry went to an "accelerated" high school. Not only did it meet later in the day, which allowed him to work full time, but he would also graduate two years early and be able to volunteer for the army at seventeen rather than wait until he was eighteen.

He joined up as soon as he was able and was assigned to the infantry. Tests were given, and he became a candidate for officer's training. In the United States, whether you went to a military academy or a university and took ROTC, you needed a college degree to be commissioned as a second lieutenant. In Israel, this was not possible. You could not attend a university unless you had served in the army. There were exceptions for disabilities, religious deferments, and some academic deferments, but otherwise you had to serve your mandatory military service first. Gerry went to officer's training school for a year and was commissioned as a second lieutenant, the youngest officer yet to serve in the Israeli army.

Gerald Drapacz, Wanda's brother, changed his last name to Harel, a more Israeli-sounding name. It was a common practice at the time and encouraged among the young and aspiring Zionists who wanted to rid themselves of their European ghetto names. His assignment after officer's training was to the Givati brigade. This was an elite unit created during the war of independence as part of the southern command to fight along the Egyptian and Gaza borders and protect the settlements in the Negev. Their purple berets, black boots, and insignia with a fox on it distinguished them from other units. They trained in the Negev desert. At the end of their basic training, they would climb Masada for their induction ceremony. Masada overlooks the desert and the Dead Sea. You can see Jordan across the sea. Every man was given a rifle and a Bible. The rallying cry was "Never Again." This was an allusion to the events at Masada between 70 and 73 AD. After the destruction of Jerusalem, a group of zealots and their families climbed up to the mountain fortress and held out against the Romans for three years. By the time the Romans breached the walls, most of the people were dead from fighting or suicide.

Masada is a symbol of the Shoah, where so many had died defenseless. They had no army of their own to protect them; they had no homeland to emigrate to, no training in how to defend themselves. Masada was also a symbol of Israel itself. Alone and isolated, surrounded by enemies, they might be forced to fight to the last man. As Golda Meir had said, "The Egyptians could run to Egypt, the Syrians into Syria. The only place we could run was into the sea, and before we did that, we might as well fight." These young recruits had been thoroughly indoctrinated and well trained so that they would give all they had and be able to say, "Never again."

At officer training school, you had to choose a general from history as a sort of mentor. Gerald liked both Patton and Rommel, but for obvious reasons he choose Patton. Patton led his men in North Africa and understood desert warfare. Like many Israelis at the time, Gerry was not fond of Eisenhower or the British. He believed, like Patton, that Eisenhower coddled the British, and this slowed down the war. Had Patton been allowed to advance as rapidly as he wanted and received the supplies he needed, he might have ended the war sooner, and the lives of as many as a million Jews might have been saved. The battles would have been bloodier, but the war would have ended sooner, saving many more lives.

Israeli officers are expected to lead from the front. Their battle cry is "After me." As a result of officers taking lead combat positions, they proportionately suffer the highest officer casualty rates in the world. Soldiers are trained to take over command when an officer is killed or injured. Unlike his contemporary, Ariel Sharon, Gerry would not make a career out of the army. During his military service, other than the Sinai campaign in 1956, he would be busy fighting the fedayeen. The key would be a rapid, nighttime assault. It was dangerous. Things can get very confused in the dark, and this was long before anyone had "night vision" technology. The advantage was that the Palestinians were unprepared for this kind of fighting. Some still wore the white kaffiyeh on their heads, which made a good target at night.

The word "fedayeen" is loosely translated as guerilla fighters. For some, the Palestinian fedayeen were freedom fighters, and for others, they were terrorists. The fedayeen were of national socialist, socialist, and communist orientation. Their stated goal was a nonsectarian, democratic state in the area formerly known as Palestine. They formed groups with different political orientations, with different leaders under independent commands, supported by different countries. They formed an umbrella organization known as the Palestine Liberation Organization (PLO). After Israeli independence, Palestinian Arabs who were forced out by Israel, or left under the urging of the grand mufti of Jerusalem, settled in refugee camps along the border with Israel in Lebanon, Syria, Jordan, and Gaza. The earliest cross-border raids were primarily economic, such as the harvesting of crops from their former villages or collecting belongings left behind. By 1953 most of these attacks targeted Israeli civilian and military targets. The Israelis began retaliatory attacks into Jordan and Gaza, where the majority of fedayeen raids stemmed from. By 1954 the Egyptians, who under the armistice agreement could not move troops into Gaza, formed the Palestinian Border Police as a cover for the fedayeen groups. Increasing attacks from Gaza, stationing Egyptian troops in Gaza, and the closure of the Straits of Tiran was the Israeli justification for the 1956 Sinai campaign.

It was in late 1954 that Gerry, now a full lieutenant, was to be part of a retaliatory strike at a police compound in Gaza at Rafah (also known as

Rafiah), along the Egyptian border. The compound was merely a cover for about 150 fedayeen. Defense Minister David Ben-Gurion personally approved the mission, and Haim Bar-Lev, brigadier general of the Givati brigade, would accompany the men. The assault was a precursor to other assaults the Israelis would make as part of a general policy of retaliation for fedayeen attacks. If the assault were successful, the lessons learned would be used in more retaliatory attacks, including a larger operation against Khan-Younis.

The atmosphere in the room at Kibbutz Nahal Oz in the Negev Desert was tense. General Bar-Lev was going over the plans for the assault. The compound was not outside Rafah but in the town. The attack was scheduled for three o'clock in the morning, when the fedayeen would be asleep, and the guards would be half-asleep. The Israelis would travel to the border in armored vehicles but cross the border on foot and march several miles in the quiet darkness. They would carry their heavy machine guns and set them up before beginning the attack. They would fight their way into the compound, set dynamite charges, and blow up the main building inside, scattering and, if necessary, killing as many of the enemy as possible.

General Bar-Lev went over the plans again with the captain and Lieutenant Harel. The captain was hesitant as they did not know the exact location of the police compound. He had reservations about the operation. His attitude did not seem gung ho enough without more exacting information. He had forgotten Moshe Dayan's command for the infantry: aggression, initiative, and ingenuity. General Bar-Lev turned to Lieutenant Harel and asked him what he thought.

"I thought you would never ask," the lieutenant replied. He would have given anything for this chance to lead men into the heart of danger. He was young and burned for battle, with little regard for his own safety. This was not war. It was a matter of revenge. Israel was a small country with a small population. It was hard not to know someone who had lost a loved one. This undeclared war was personal for the Israelis and the Palestinians. The Palestinians wanted to turn back the clock.

The Israelis would not go back. The fedayeen incursions were becoming bolder and more frequent. They were armed and financed by Egypt's dictator, Nasser.

Nasser cared little for the lives of the Palestinians. He wanted the Americans and the Russians to vie for the chance to give him unlimited weapons and aid. To be taken seriously, he needed to be the leader of the Arab world. He fomented rebellion against the leaders of Iraq and Jordan. He financed the Algerian rebellion against France. He needed to be the most anti-Zionist leader of all the nations of the Middle East. He broadcast his message of not just defeating Israel but also annihilating the population.

The general put Lieutenant Harel in charge of the assault operation. General Bar-Lev expected to accompany the unit. Lieutenant Harel told him he could not come as long as the general put him in charge of the operation. The general would only be in the way, and the lieutenant would have to assign three or four soldiers to guard him. Gerald did not need a general looking over his shoulder. He looked at the general and said, "Who is in charge here?"

Lieutenant Gerald Harel led his men on the road to Rafah. It was deadly quiet, and he prayed that it stayed that way. As he entered Rafah, he quickly found the police compound. Inside were about 130 fedayeen. During the march, he thought only of his mission, to put an end to the enemy's operations, with as few casualties as possible. The Israeli army had a policy of bringing home all their men, dead or alive. They left none of their own to the enemy. Minimizing casualties was important. They had few men to waste. The wounded and dead were not mere "casualties." They were friends and relatives.

The men quietly set up their heavy machine guns. Gerald led a company of 120 men. They were divided into platoons of thirty men each and squads of ten men each. They were all disciplined soldiers. When everyone was in position, Gerald gave the order to fire. The fedayeen were taken completely by surprise. If they thought they were safe in Gaza, then they had made a terrible mistake. A platoon breached the compound. The soldiers planted their explosives and pulled back. The explosion lit up the darkness. Bodies flew through the air along with the concrete. Lieutenant Harel led his soldiers into the compound, firing their Uzis while the heavy machine guns provided cover fire.

At this point, it was no longer personal. It was soldiers in the act of performing their mission. Some fedayeen ran away. Most of them were not so lucky. The Israelis had gone in fast and hard. The entire firefight took less than a half hour. Four Israelis were lightly wounded. They gathered up their weapons and disappeared into the darkness out of Rafah. A squad was organized to guard the rear of their small column against the counterattack that never came.

Twenty

CALL ME DAVID

*Suffering makes a people greater, and we have suffered much.
We had a message to give the world, but we were overwhelmed,
and the message was cut off in the middle. In time
there will be millions of us—becoming stronger and
stronger—and we will complete the message.*

—DAVID BEN-GURION

H e paced back and forth for several hours in the briefing room. He was short, stocky, and bald, with untrimmed white hair sticking out from the sides of his head. His face was creased from the sun and his age. His name was David Ben-Gurion, and he was Israel's founding father. He helped write Israel's Declaration of Independence in 1948 and was the first to sign it. He had been the first Prime Minister of Israel. He stepped down in 1954 to become defense minister. He could not tolerate not being in charge, so he would return as prime minister in only one year. It did not matter whether he was defense minister or prime minister; he would have been there either way.

Ben-Gurion came to Palestine in 1906 as a committed Zionist. He had not suffered persecution in his home in Russian-occupied Poland.

He did not run away. He came to build a Jewish homeland. His first fight was with Arabs who tried to rob the farm where he was working in 1909. In 1912 he moved to Istanbul to study law. He split from other Zionists in believing their future lay within the Turkish Empire. Back in Palestine, he formed a militia in 1915 to support the Ottoman troops against the British. He went to America to raise an army of ten thousand men to fight for the Ottomans. In 1917, after the British published the Balfour Declaration, he changed sides and joined the Palestinian brigade of the British Army, believing in their promise of a Jewish homeland. When the British broke their promises, he came to realize that the Jews would have to rely on their own military ingenuity if they were to create their own state. By 1933 he had risen to become the leader of the Yishuv and took his seat at the League of Nations. He replaced Haim Arlosoroff, who was murdered by right-wing Zionists.

Ben-Gurion believed there was room for accommodation with the Arabs. He became a man of the desert, believing that it was the most promising area of Jewish settlement where they would not be in conflict with the Arabs. To the young people who wanted to be pioneers, he would tell them, "Golden youth, go to the Negev." He made his home in the Negev at Kibbutz Sde Boker.

This is where Gerry met him the second time. The first time was when Gerry was a young recruit. Ben-Gurion personally met all the new recruits. Israeli army units were rotated as guards for him when he was on the kibbutz. At night, he would sit with the soldiers. They would light a fire, make coffee, bake potatoes in the fire, and sing. He would talk about Greek philosophy until his wife would finally call to him in Yiddish to go to bed.

He loved being with his young soldiers. He knew the nation could not survive without them. He had been the one to gather the various independent fighting groups and form them into a national army. He had to deal with a wide number of political factions and the religious Jews in order to form a loyal, democratic government. From his teenage years until the end of his life, he was a committed Zionist and socialist.

He believed in equality and giving everyone the right to work the land. The informality and egalitarianism of the Israeli army and the degree of fraternization between officers and soldiers was part of that belief. An Israeli veteran once told me that if you see a soldier or officer walking down the street with only one or two medals, he was a big hero. They don't give out a lot of medals. Everyone is expected to do his duty. That was a part of Ben-Gurion's legacy.

When Lieutenant Harel came into the room, still full of the adrenaline of battle and the excitement of success, Ben-Gurion and Bar-Lev had wide smiles. They had already been informed of the success of the operation. Bar-Lev admitted that Gerald was right in not allowing him to accompany the men. Gerald addressed him the defense minister as Mr. Ben-Gurion, but Ben-Gurion said, "Call me David." This was the way it was with the old man. He wanted to know every detail. Ben-Gurion personally served the coffee and pastries and peppered Gerry with questions. They talked for a few hours. The group broke up, and the newly appointed Captain Harel headed back to his army base.

By 1955 Nasser was attempting to rule Egypt under a variety of unsettling conditions such as preventing coups and assassination attempts. Eisenhower was trying to convince the Arabs and Israelis to form a NATO-like organization known as the Middle East Defense Organization ("MEDO"). The United States wanted a peaceful Middle East and feared Soviet penetration. To that end, the United States was willing to supply weapons to all parties, provided there was a balance of power that would prevent any party from being able to destroy the other. Nasser could not comprehend the threat from the Soviets, who were far away, when the British still had forces in the canal zone that he feared could be used to overthrow him. The geopolitical concerns of the United States were considered secondary to Nasser. His first concern was dealing with former colonial powers of Britain and France. Egyptian and Soviet support for the Algerians as they fought for their independence from France, sent the French looking for an ally in the region.

France's nuclear development program needed help. Israel had a cadre of brilliant physicists who sought a nuclear program for both energy production and a nuclear deterrent capability, should all conventional means of defense fail. By 1955 the two governments had developed a close relationship. France saw a stable, democratic ally in Israel and committed herself to securing Israel's survival. When Egypt finally started receiving weapons from the communist bloc, the balance of power tilted against Israel. France supplied Israel with weapons and aircraft, changing that balance. The Franco-Israeli unofficial alliance would continue until 1967.

The British eventually withdrew its troops from the Suez Canal zone with the provision that they could return if the canal's safety was threatened. Nasser closed the canal to Israeli passage and also closed the Straits of Tiran, preventing Israeli shipping commerce from using its Red Sea port of Eilat. Egypt also violated the 1948 armistice agreement by concentrating thousands of troops in Gaza. These acts, along with Nasser's determination to become the leader of the Arabs by constantly threatening Israel's destruction, convinced the Israeli leadership that war was their only option. Israel believed if they could capture the Sinai, they could open the Straits of Tiran and negotiate a peace treaty with Egypt in return for the Sinai.

Captain Gerald Harel volunteered to stay in the army an additional six months after his enlistment was up. In a letter to General Bar-Lev, he asked to be transferred inland to a training camp so that he could live off the base and start attending classes at the Hebrew University in Jerusalem. Though Bar-Lev was reluctant to lose a good officer, he granted Gerry's request. When his enlistment was over, he became a part of the reserves, as did all former soldiers. They were called up for training and active duty for one month every year. Israel relied on a small standing army of draftees with provisions for rapid mobilization of the reserves when necessary.

Like so many former Israeli soldiers I have talked to, Gerry said his military service was the happiest time of his life. The camaraderie with other young men who had a shared purpose, having friends from high school who were wounded or killed fighting for the same goals, and the close relationships between officers and soldiers is not easily appreciated by those who have not had the experience.

Gerry enjoyed removing his officer's insignia from his uniform and sitting with the soldiers in the mess hall. He looked so young, they assumed he was a new recruit. They would tease him and call him "fresh meat." Only later, when they met him on the training ground, would they realize their mistake and beg forgiveness. For Gerry it was just a good-hearted joke and typical of the relationship he had with his soldiers.

Fate would bring Gerry one last chance to fight for his country. The British, French, and Israelis developed a secret plan to attack Egypt and hopefully topple Nasser. The French were furious at Nasser for his interference in Algeria and compared him to Hitler. His desire for power seemed insatiable, and neither the British nor the French wanted another appeasement like Munich. Nikita Khrushchev promised the French that the Soviets and the Egyptians would withdraw their support for the Algerian rebellion if France would withdraw from NATO. The French refused to betray their allies and so believed that the United States would support them. The British feared Nasser would disrupt shipping through the canal. His refusal to allow Israeli vessels through was a violation of international agreements, and no one knew who his next target would be.

The plan was for Israel to invade the Sinai up to the canal. With opposing forces on both sides of the canal, the French and British would be entitled to seize the canal in order to protect any disruption in international shipping. British and Israeli relations were no better than the British and American relations after American independence. The Israelis distrusted the British, and the British had no confidence in the Israelis' fighting ability. The French brought the two together at a series of secret meetings in Sevres, where they formed their tripartite pact.

The Israeli plan was to first strike at Gaza City, where thousands of Egyptian soldiers were preparing to invade Israel. The Israelis would strike from the north with a small unit of tanks that would act as mobile artillery. Captain Harel led a much smaller group and positioned them on a hill to the south of Gaza City where he would prevent Egyptian reinforcements from entering the city. Harel's job was to launch a fake assault on the Egyptians with his force, hoping the Egyptians would face him and believe this was the main attack. The main Israeli force would attack from the north and smash into the Egyptians' rear, causing confusion and enveloping the larger Egyptian forces.

As in all wars, a mistake was made. The main force launched its attack before notifying Harel. Egyptian soldiers now faced the main Israeli force, a force that was only one quarter the size of the Egyptian force bearing down on them. The Israeli main force was now in danger of being destroyed in a conventional battle.

Captain Harel immediately understood the danger. Without orders and on his own initiative, he committed his men to a downhill assault on the Egyptian rear. Had the Egyptians understood the size of Harel's unit, it would not have been a problem. The ferocity and speed of the attack, combined with the confusion it created when the Egyptians were being fired upon from behind, led to the rapid destruction of the Egyptian forces. Only a few would escape the envelopment. The victory was complete. The Israelis would open the Straits of Tiran and capture the Sinai up to the canal where the British and French would secure the vital waterway.

Captain Harel was now Major Harel, the youngest major in the Israeli army. He would receive a letter of commendation and a small medal for his initiative in Gaza City. The Americans and British were surprised at the Israelis' fighting ability and realized they were the most powerful and stable force in the Middle East. Britain would withdraw its officers from the Jordanian army. The joy of their victory soon turned bitter in the mouths of Major Harel and the State of Israel as the United States would force them to withdraw from Sinai without any concessions from Egypt.

While the American and Israeli governments have cooperated and supported each other, they live in different neighborhoods and sometimes view the strategic situation quite differently. The Israelis focus on their national survival. The Americans look at larger geopolitical goals—and this was true about the Sinai campaign. Eisenhower was upset with the lack of consultation by the British, French, and Israelis in launching the war only one week before his reelection. One of his life's missions in becoming president was finding common ground with the Soviets in order to lessen tensions and so bring about a safer and more peaceful world. At the same time, the Egyptians were still nonaligned. He hoped to woo Nasser into the American camp with nonmilitary aid for economic development. The Sinai campaign threw a wrench into the works, and Eisenhower demanded a withdrawal of all foreign troops.

Eisenhower finished his time in office without achieving either of his goals. Nasser wanted military aid more than economic development, something that Eisenhower would not provide. He turned to the Soviets for help. Nasser was a young lieutenant in 1948. He experienced the frustration of other officers in the war. Bullets and rifles did not match. Tanks broke down. Even their maps were hopelessly inaccurate. They had no idea how to get to Tel Aviv. He formed a revolutionary council that eventually overthrew King Farouk's government in 1952.

Nasser was obsessed with removing the stain of defeat by a people whom he considered a mere vestige of the colonialist powers of Britain and France, who for so long had degraded and oppressed the Egyptian and Arab peoples. His government was a national socialist totalitarian regime. He built Radio Cairo, the largest tower in the Middle East, from which he could broadcast his virulent anti-Semitic diatribes directly to the people of the region and even undermine and foment rebellion against those Arab leaders who did not agree with him. He would send aid and even troops to foment rebellion in Iraq, Yemen, and Jordan. He was obsessed with his hatred and distrust of the former colonial powers, and he would never give up his attempts to destroy Israel for the rest of his life.

The memory of the Sinai Campaign of 1956 was lost between the war of independence in 1948 and the 1967 war. It is, however, an important part of Israeli history. The 1950s were Israel's formative years. It was a critical period that would determine whether Israel would survive or be crushed by the huge armies arrayed against it. An army and its tactics were formed. A new society was created. The population more than doubled. Immigrants came from around the world, and a poor country, with few resources, had to be forged into a nation with the common goal of survival. The desert had to be irrigated. Great men and women guided this painful birth. Men like Haim Bar-Lev, Moshe Dayan, Ariel Sharon, and Gerald Harel led men into battle and fought to protect a young nation so that it could grow and ensure its continued existence.

Twenty-One

My Lai: Sam Bruner

"**Y**ou need a haircut. Not everyone has long hair. You shouldn't stand out. Find other ways to be exceptional if you want to stand out from the crowd," my father said for the umpteenth time. Dinnertime in the early 1970s had become routine. The main subject was either the length of Joe's hair or mine, or the Vietnam War. Vietnam was not just a war issue; it involved politics, demonstrations, and rebellion by what my father saw as spoiled children who had no idea what America stood for, the true ugliness of communism, and the naïveté of not believing we were in a war with the Soviet Union. He said no nation was perfect, but when measured against others, given the amount of our power, America was still the most restrained and important country in the world.

I guess he was not happy with our opinions. He was at least partly to blame. Like many survivors, he was obsessed with current events. At work, news radio played all day long. At dinnertime, he spun the TV around to watch the news while we ate before he went back to the store. We were discussing the news and post–World War II history regularly. I became a news and politics hound at a young age. I always respected my father's opinion and assumed he was right about things, but in time, I became a teenager and started to form my own ideas. This was something he was never ready for. I don't know why. It was as though he could not remember what it was like to be young.

I was most fascinated as a child with watching the civil rights demonstrations on TV. That was one form of government disobedience that both my parents supported. Dad sometimes asked me what I wanted to do when I grew up. I remember telling him I wanted to be a lawyer and work for Martin Luther King so I could help his people be free. He laughed. He said it was good to be liberal at a young age. He was all for equality under the law, but he also told me there was no way that people would get along unless they wanted to. He always said that people never really change. Maybe individuals would change, but human behavior would always be the same. People would find their differences, and one group would always try to be on top. I am sure he thought we should be raised with a healthy dose of cynicism for our own good.

"American soldiers don't do such things," my father said, and my mother echoed, "If they did anything wrong, such things happen in wars. Mistakes are made. If it were the Russians or the Chinese, you would see real slaughter." A point well taken but unappreciated until years later when the Russians invaded Afghanistan and Chechnya. "You have no idea what war is. Men get tired and confused. The enemy is mixed in with the civilians. On top of that, they are fighting in the jungles."

First it was the Tet offensive that brought about the "credibility gap" and brought down Lyndon Johnson. Now it was the My Lai massacre, where American soldiers killed innocent civilians, and the outpouring of similar stories by veterans that caused so many more Americans to question our involvement in Vietnam. My parents could not accept the fact that these soldiers were not the same soldiers who fought in World War II. As my father often said, people don't really change. It was the situation that was different. There were draft rotations instead of fighting for the duration. Draft deferments abounded for men enrolled in college. I had teachers who freely admitted they had become teachers to avoid the draft. At home, we were building the Great Society and having a good old time. No one was suffering except for some brown-skinned people in a far-off place. I am not so strident now, or as sure of my opinions about Vietnam, but it was not World War II.

Politics was another area where my parents were different from native American Jews. Most Jews voted for Adlai Stevenson. My parents voted for Eisenhower. He was a great man to them. American Jews did not suffer as European Jews had, so they had no idea about Eisenhower's greatness. Only Eisenhower would know how to deal with the Russians.

"What about the Rosenbergs? What about McCarthyism? Clearly, Jews were targeted. There was no precedent for executing the Rosenbergs. There was never enough evidence against them. Eisenhower could have stopped the execution. Eisenhower refused to denounce McCarthy until the army was attacked," I stated one evening during one of our many political discussions.

"The Rosenbergs may not have been guilty, but they were dirty, and so were a lot of those other people," my mother told me. They had no pity. Being a communist was the same as working for the Russians. As Jews, we were supposed to conduct ourselves in a manner that did not bring discredit to our people. Decades later, they felt no different about Bernie Madoff. They should throw the book at him. He should have been an example for people to admire the Jews, instead of feeding stereotypes.

One night after dinner, when I was sixteen or seventeen and thinking about college, my father asked me why I wanted to go to college. I told him I wanted to help change things, and the best way was law and politics. He told me that he knew a few lawyers, and he did not think I would make a very good one. Why he would want to crush such dreams, I did not know. He believed business was the best profession, and being self-employed was the highest aspiration. You could hire all the lawyers, engineers, and other professionals you needed. Business was the central hub around which everything else evolved. Were it not for business, all other professions would have no means of employment. It was a fair argument, but he could not understand that people have different talents and goals. My mother was not in favor of his attitude, even though she agreed with his basic philosophy.

In time, I gained some understanding of my father's reasons for disdaining higher education. Upon their arrival in New York, my parents became quickly disenchanted. They were used to the tree-lined boulevards and orderliness of European cities. To them, New York was a jungle and no place to raise children. On top of that, it was an island. In case of an emergency—and nuclear war was a real threat at the time—you would not be able to get away with all those people trying to cross bridges. Jewish communities in the United States were willing to help refugee families. My parents moved to Des Moines, Iowa.

They were in the American heartland and only knew a few words of English. The Jewish community helped him find a job. They paid the rent on a house for a few months and gave them food and clothing for Harry and Joe. People were kind to my parents, and my mother made friends easily. My father was working for the Army Corps of Engineers as a draftsman. Engineers designed things, and draftsmen drew the components. In Russia, they trained you to do a specific job and called you an engineer after a minimal education. In America, you had to have a college degree. He could not understand the need for a broad theoretical background. All you needed was enough knowledge to do the job. He believed he could do the same work that the engineers were doing, but he had no degree, and he had not the time, money, or inclination to go to college. He was resentful. He quit and got a job as a watchmaker at a Zales jewelry store. He wanted to start his own business and try to market the calendar watchband again.

Among my favorite classes in high school was English. It had always been history and social studies, but in tenth grade, I had a teacher named Mr. Shelly. We read *The Crucible.* We discussed its modern meaning and the comparison to McCarthyism. He also had us read a few more radical books, including *Manchild in the Promised Land,* a raw, detailed account of growing up in Harlem. That book landed him in trouble. Some parents complained, and he had to stop teaching that book. He brought his guitar into class, stood on his desk, and sang "The Times They Are A-Changin'." He was not re-hired the next year.

In eleventh grade, I met Bruce Marcoon. He was hip. He had long hair. He wore an American flag vest. He connected with teenagers. He was cool. Unfortunately, the first half of the year was English mechanics. I never liked learning grammar, the parts of speech, and, worst of all, diagramming sentences. I was bored. I sat in the back, bored and joking around. Most teachers would just slap you with a few detentions. Bruce pulled me aside after class and basically told me to shape up or he would request that I be removed from the class. I shaped up and started to listen. By the second half of the year, we were reading literature. *Moby-Dick* became the book that opened my mind to great literature. It taught me to understand the many levels of meaning that a writer could use. I began to look at literature, poetry, and even people's actions in a different way. It was not a revelation that came all at once. It became a guide that grew more important with time as I grew.

Decades later, during a family trek through New England, we stopped in New Bedford. We toured a whaling ship and a whaling museum, and we even sat in the pew of the church that Melville attended and wrote about. We found a book about the *Essex.* It was a whaling ship that sank when it was rammed by a large sperm whale. Some of the crew got away in the boats. They were stranded at sea. Hunger and thirst drove them mad. First, they ate the dead. In time, they drew lots and sacrificed one another. Eventually, the captain was rescued. As his boat came alongside the rescue ship, he was holding onto the bones of shipmates and chewing them. Eventually, his sanity returned. He became captain of another ship. In his quarters, he had a net hung from the ceiling and kept it loaded with food.

I thought about my parents. The freezer was always full, and the cabinets were stuffed with canned goods. My father explained to me that you never knew when there could be upheavals, war, or revolution. It was comforting to know there was enough food around to survive for at least a few weeks. If you rationed it carefully, it could last for months. Along with food, I was told I should always keep a current passport, some cash, and jewelry.

As I was now unsure of college, and my father was unwilling to help, I became confused about my future and even depressed. As I was leaving class one day, Bruce came over to me and asked if something was wrong. I wasn't the same person, and if I wanted to see him after school to talk, he would be there. I came by later, and after some probing, I finally told him my father said I shouldn't go to college. Bruce said, "Your father is wrong." These four simple words from a stranger gave me the courage to believe in myself. Of course, there was more discussion and words of support, but those few words were burned into my memory the way the Ten Commandments were carved into the tablets.

I have heard that a good parent is someone who believes in his child when the child does not believe in himself. Never mind that college was a great experience that opened up many areas of learning and broadened my horizons. Forget about the fact that decades later, when I did decide to go to law school, it would not have been a realistic endeavor had I not already had a bachelor's degree. Here was a stranger who saw something in me that my father did not. He saw something of value in me at a time when I saw so little. Later I would have a meeting with my guidance counselor, Mr. Abrams. I told him this story. He called my mother and told her that he had been the guidance counselor for all four of her children, and that if any of them should go to college, it should be me. My mother hounded my father, and he left me alone after that.

In 2015 my brother died, my father died, my mother-in-law was diagnosed with lung cancer, and I watched my mother slip into dementia. I felt a need to reconnect with many people. I searched the Internet to find Bruce. I realized that I had never thanked him for his intervention or expressed what it meant to me. He related a story about another student several years before. She had some family problems and would stop by after school to talk to him. One day she went to see him after school. He had to go to a faculty meeting and asked her to wait. When he came back, she was gone. That night she committed suicide. After that, he decided not to put off helping a student that he thought was in trouble. As my father always said, it was a matter of destiny.

Twenty-Two

Back in the USA

My mother loved American music—Nat King Cole, Elvis Presley, Woody Guthrie, and the Everly Brothers. It reminded her of all her memories of America. Not only did she teach me the theme song from *Casablanca* as a young child, she was always singing "Red River Valley."

She told me of a time she was visiting Aunt Helen and Uncle Jacob in Missouri. I wasn't born yet, and neither was Helen's youngest son, Eric. Mom brought Harry and Joe with her for the visit. At some point, Helen had to go out. Mom was home alone with Abe and Mike (Helen's sons), along with Joe and Harry. The boys were running around the house, yelling and driving my mother nuts. She also wanted Joe and Mike to take a nap. Finally, she sat them all down to play a game. The one who could teach her the best song was the winner. They all stood up to sing a song. Abe was the last one. He stood up in his red cowboy hat and sang "Red River Valley."

She sang that song to me over and over through the years as I sat next to her on the sofa. She did not have all the words right, so I learned to sing it for her. As my mother got older, and my father passed, I thought about my mother's mortality and the words "for they say you have taken the sunshine that has brightened our lives for a while." She treated so many nieces and nephews almost as they were her own children.

Now I was not in America. I was in a condo in Tel Aviv and if Uncle Jacob slapped me one more time on the left arm, I would surely scream. I had left after work on Kibbutz Ma'ale Hachamisha near Jerusalem. I took the bus into town and walked to a clinic, where I got my yellow-fever vaccine for my trip to India. I had a World Health Organization card that listed all the vaccines I needed and this was the last one. I walked several miles back to the bus station and boarded a bus for Tel Aviv. Because Jerusalem is in the hills, the bus had to climb and descend in low gear. The buses were not quite as modern as the ones in the United States, so the loud groaning of the transmission could give a normal person a headache. By the time I got off the bus in Tel Aviv, I had a fever, a headache, and a very sore red bump on my left arm where I had gotten the yellow-fever shot. I took a local bus and still had to walk several miles to an apartment building.

It was standard housing in Tel Aviv: a poured concrete building with small two- and three-bedroom apartments. Most were purchased as condos. That was the Israeli dream of owning your own home. Life wasn't easy. Income taxes on the middle class were extremely high. Sales taxes on imported goods (most major purchases were imported) could double or triple the price of the item. It was not uncommon for people to work two jobs. My father did that years earlier in the United States, but only until he could get the store to bring in enough income. Here, you might do it as long as you had a family to support.

When I got to the apartment, Uncle Jacob and Aunt Helen were there. They were staying with Jacob's cousin and his wife. His cousin was his only living relative. Jacob had saved for a long time for this trip. He seemed so happy to finally be in Israel. I am sure he would have stayed if he could.

This family was a typical Israeli family. They had two sons. The younger one was my age. He was serving in the military. There is a three-year draft, and it is compulsory for most Israeli men. (It is also compulsory for most Israeli women, but they serve less than two years.) His name was David. He was very nice to me and interested in what I planned to do. He was already tired of the army routine. He had been in the tank corps and hurt his back. Unlike other armies, where you would be discharged for a permanent injury, you did not get off so easy in the Israeli army. They made him a photographer and personal aide to a high-ranking officer. He was, like many Israelis I met, jumpy, nervous, fast-talking, and chain-smoking. He searched his room for anything he could find to help me on my trip—a canteen, mess kit, even a pair of army boots—but I really did not need anything. They had another, older son. He had taken a piece of shrapnel in the leg. That leg was shorter. He wore an elevated shoe and walked with a limp.

This was the situation in so many Israeli families. You were supposed to be proud to serve in the army. You were proud to do your duty. It was a great socializing force that required Jews of so many different backgrounds to get along. It was all about pride until you were hurt. Parents were worried about their sons and daughters in the military just like in the United States, except the threat of harm was constant. Now that her son was wounded, the mother was not so kindly in her speech about the army. Like other wounded soldiers, David received little help or money from the army. They just did not have it to give. David was, like other Israelis I met who were my age, envious of my position. I had the freedom and money to travel, while he was stuck in the army for three years.

I had come to pick up some money, money that I had earned working the night shift at Acme Bakeries in Philadelphia after high school. I had paid for my airfare, took a few hundred dollars with me, and left about eight hundred dollars with my mother, who sent it via American Express when I needed it. I had not spent much while living on the kibbutz. Most of my needs were taken care of. I hitchhiked with friends and took buses around the country, staying in youth hostels and eating very cheaply from street vendors. I asked my mother to send me another four hundred dollars for my trip to India. My parents were less than thrilled with the idea of their eighteen-year-old son traveling overland to India through so many Muslim countries. I did not have their hard-earned wartime experiences, and they feared for my life. I was going with several

British friends. European kids were much more used to such travel, and India was not a strange place at all to them.

In a last attempt to dissuade me, my parents gave the money to Aunt Helen. I was forced to go to Tel Aviv in an attempt to retrieve it. Helen tried her best. It is not that other mothers do not worry about their children. That is their job, it seems; but it is common for survivors to be even more worried. They lost so much. They were unhappy if we lived more than an hour or two away. Although America is a very mobile country, it seems that most of my cousins and siblings stayed close to home. First Aunt Helen worked me over. As David was in the army, she assumed he was more mature and levelheaded than me. She asked him if he would go to India. He said he would go with me if it weren't for the army. She told me that people would kill me for my boots. David ran into his room and brought out two pairs of army boots. He said I could have them and give them away so I would not be short of boots. Aunt Helen handed me the money and told me I had better write my mother every day. I understood my mother's worry, so I wrote her every other day.

Jacob talked to me for several hours. I think he was trying to wear me down. He was trying to be my friend. When I sat down at the table, he gave me a tap on my left arm, right on the vaccination site. The pain shot through me. My headache worsened. He told me about the Russian army. He told me about going into house-to-house combat, shooting first and looking for prisoners later, if anyone survived, and of course, fighting in the winter where men lost their legs from the cold. He talked about being eighteen and looking for adventure, how hard he worked for the Zionists on a kibbutz, and preparing to go to Palestine. He did understand me in many ways.

He was a good man, and I knew he was trying to look out for me. He understood what I was looking for. His voice was gentle, but like many of his generation, his eyes were piercing. I had always liked him. When my mother and father were fighting and threatening divorce while I was in high school, he came over and listened to my mother. He did not lecture her or argue with her. He agreed that my father was a difficult man.

He was a good listener, and that is what my mother needed. These were good-hearted, hard-working people. I do not know what their home life was like, but I suspect that Helen and Jacob were quite devoted to each other.

When Uncle Jacob was finished talking to me, he said, "OK, Sam," and patted me on the left arm. I told him not to do that, but I don't think he heard me. When I did not relent, he talked awhile longer and patted me on the arm some more. I thought I would faint at that point. I got up to leave. I hugged Aunt Helen, shook Uncle Jacob's hand, and said good-bye to David. I walked to the bus stop, went to the bus terminal, and rode the bus to Jerusalem while the transmission ground away. I took a bus to the kibbutz and walked to my room, where I collapsed.

When I thought about the young Israelis I met, I almost felt guilty for being a spoiled American. They worked hard, higher education was not as widely available as it was in the United States, and there were fewer job opportunities. Yet, they seemed not to be bored and were able to suck more of the juice out of life. They seemed to get more fun out of the little things. In the United States, the draft rules had changed. There was a lottery system, and you were only eligible while you were nineteen. The Vietnam war was winding down. They were drafting far fewer men, yet my number was high up on the list. I had decided that should I be called, I would rather join the Israeli army and serve my time in a more helpful fashion than going to Vietnam and possibly being one of the last to die in a lost cause. Fortunately, I was not called up. Had I been in the Israeli army, I would have been caught up in the 1973 Yom Kippur War and probably wishing I was in Vietnam.

The pressure was always on when I was in Israel. I do not know how many Israelis told me the nation could use a young man like me, how the army needed me. Personally, I felt like the army needed cannon fodder, not me in particular. As much as I wanted to be sucked in, something inside me always made me feel like an American first. For me, I never felt more like an American than when I was away from home. Maybe that was just because my family was there, but there was more. I had been born and raised there, and while I was reminded that I was a Jew, I also knew that was part of being an American as much as any other minority. Also, in America, all options were on the table. I could be or do anything. The sense of limitless freedom and opportunity would always draw me to America. Whenever I was away, I could not wait for the jet to land on American soil.

As a "Trekkie" and sci-fi fan, I often wonder about alternate time-lines. There are innumerable paths that you can choose from in your actions as a young person, but you can only follow one. What would the path have been if I had been as focused as some of my peers and gone straight to college and graduate school? Would I have been an unhappy lawyer wishing I had gone into the jewelry business with my brother? As my wife, Jesse, and I traveled through Israel when Jesse was thirteen, I often wondered what my life would have been like had I stayed in Israel and joined the army. I will never know whether I took the right path. I can only look at the woman I married and the sons we have raised. I am thoroughly grateful for those choices, and they are the most important choices I could have made. Like *Candide*, I can only say that this must be the best of all possible worlds, because it is the one I have chosen to live. I have no regrets.

Twenty-Three

No Regrets

Guilt is useless.
Regrets are only helpful if we have
something to learn from them.

—Dr. Mary Hebblewhite, paraphrasing
the teachings of the Buddha

I looked at him as he lay in his casket. He had no regrets. He was sorry for nothing. He finally had nothing to say. The raging bull was silent. He had cheated death so many times, for so long a time, but now his time was over. My wife, Deb, was a clinical cancer nurse for many years. She had watched a lot of people die slowly. She had plenty of time to observe them. She concluded, after many years, that people die as they have lived. If they were narcissistic and demanding, cowardly, or brave and always thinking of others, that is how they would spend their last days.

This was true of my father. He was stoic and unafraid up to the end. He did everything he could to hang on, including over two years of dialysis that his doctors said would be so debilitating he would not be able to take it for long. He did not give in to pain. He would not let go of life.

183

His mind and iron will were keeping him alive far longer than his body should have.

Joe had done a good job preplanning his funeral. If only Joe had not died four months earlier, perhaps we could have talked about how we felt. Now I felt alone. I felt sad and sorry for my mother, who had been under Dad's thumb most of her life but had become so dependent and so used to his mental abuse that she missed him and was lost without him. His story was at the end. His dominating presence that was so strong, even when he was sick and weak, still lingered. His mind was clear up to the end. He raged against the dying of the light to the very end.

Had he been overwhelmed with grief at the death of his son, I would have felt more for him. Had he said that he would rather have died than his son, as my mother had, as King David had, as any loving parent would, I would have felt more grief over my father's end. I was sad he was gone, but not anywhere near as sad and broken as when I lost my brother. I could not cry, for he had lived a long life—and lived most of it on his own terms. It simply was his time. There were no regrets for either of us. No unfinished business. No matters unresolved. I had tried my best to come to terms with him during his last ten years or so. I wanted to make sure I would not feel any lingering anger. I wanted to be sure we had said all that we had to say to each other. I had done that. This was the easy part. There would be no more trying, no more anger about the past, no more wishing that things could have been different.

My mother did not like being with old people because she did not like feeling old. After retirement, she began working out at a gym. She went at night. I asked her why she did not go during the day. Her answer was simple: only old people go during the day. She liked to go at night and be with the younger crowd. A few years earlier, my parents had booked a cruise to Antarctica. According to Mom, only old people cruise to Antarctica. For people who like to go on cruises, they end up at Antarctica when they are old because they have cruised everywhere else. Mom complained that everyone onboard was old. Never mind that my mother was in her late seventies. She moved too fast for the others. When my parents finally moved to a life-care community, some women called her the teenager. She walked three miles a day outside in good weather and bad. She took belly dancing lessons. She had lots of friends. Being around her made others feel younger.

To get on the cruise, they had to fly to Rio. It was a long flight. My father had congestive heart disease. Only one kidney was working, and it was marginal. He stopped taking his diuretics so he would not have to find a bathroom every half hour. He really wanted to enjoy this last cruise, and he did not care if it cost him his life. I was sure I would never see him again and tried to talk him out of it, but it was no use.

He came by the store to say hello, ask how business was, and look through my mail, a habit of his to which I never objected, no matter how intrusive and inappropriate it was. I was used to him. He stood around for a while as though he had something to tell me. Finally, he just shook my hand and said he would see me in two weeks. He left the store, and it only took a moment for the thought to flash through my head that I would not see him again, and I had to tell him something. I ran out of the store. He was parked just a few yards away. I yelled for him, but his hearing was bad. I caught up to him as he opened the car door. He turned partway around at my yelling. He was a good bit shorter than me. I spun him around, put my arms around him, hugged him, and told him that I loved him. He did not know how to react. He was stiff in my arms and seemed quite shocked. He never did know how to hug his child or express real emotion. He was not used to a display of affection. It did not matter. I had never told him that I loved him. I just wanted to make sure that I told him at least once, so that when he was lying in his coffin I could tell myself that I had not neglected to tell him I loved him. It was one less regret I would have. Of course, he came back from his trip just fine and lived on for a number of years.

It occurred to me during my father's funeral that I had some ups and downs with my own sons. They might be too young to recognize that someday I would be lying in a casket, and they might have regrets that would bother them if any issues between us went on too long. Sometimes the parent just has to make the move even when he feels he is right. It is not the parent who will suffer in the long run. Notwithstanding the tragic death of a child, the parent will be dead, and the child will go on for years, wondering if things could have been different. I vowed that I would not allow it to happen to my sons.

I was at peace with my father. That is not to say that we were getting along, only that I was content in knowing that I had done what I could. The bond between parent and child is special and enduring, whether that relationship is good or bad. How else can we understand loyalty, forgiveness, mercy, or love? How can we as individuals, or as a society, endure if we allow the parent-child bond to be severed?

In the Torah, a person's age is usually mentioned usually when he or she dies. The date of a person's birth is never mentioned. There is only one reference to a birthday celebration. It is in Genesis and mentions the Pharaoh's birthday. The sages tell us this is because a person is like a tree. Its life cannot be measured until it has fallen. We can never know the full measure of the person—what he or she has achieved and where he or she has failed—until he or she dies.

My father was born in 1920, when the Roaring Twenties were start-ing. Poland was free and growing economically. Cars and horses mixed on the road. The telephone was the latest thing in technology. During my father's lifetime, there would be World War II, the Shoah, the Cold War, the Berlin blockade, and a life in America. He would witness the birth of Israel, the fear of nuclear war in 1963, and the landing of a man on the moon; and by the end, he would be using a computer for word processing and Skype.

I bought a camera for his computer. I used an emulation program to dial into his computer. I would start Skype on his computer, log off, and then call from my computer. Deb and I were talking to Mom and

Dad when he started to grab his chest. He said he was in pain and that we should talk to Mom for a while. He took out the nitroglycerin tablets that he popped like Tic Tacs. I was sure I was watching him die while on Skype. After a few minutes, he felt better and started talking again. That was Dad right up until the end.

He did an amazing job of surviving the war, helping his siblings get to Berlin, and getting the necessary paperwork. The skills that he needed to survive the camps and "make it" in America were not necessarily the skills needed to make a peaceful world for him. They were not the skills needed to have a good marriage, a good family life, or a relaxing retirement. The skills he needed to make a lot of money were not the skills he needed to manage his money. The skills he needed to save his life were not the skills he needed to manage his life. He was physically and mentally abusive with his family, and to a great extent, he inherited the wind. It would be a cheap shot just to leave it at that. He had the makings of greatness. He just did not know how to put the parts together, like a watch where all the parts work in unison.

Not all of the survivors were abusers or engaged in domestic violence. For this, he has to take responsibility. There is forgiveness, but there is no excuse. It will never be known how much of the survivors' personalities are the result of their prewar lives. For people like my father, who did not believe in God, he found no evidence in the camps to change his mind. Yet, I have read accounts of observant Jews who found evidence of God in the worst of the camps. For many, it was a matter of what they believed before the war, but for others, their opinions were either formed or seriously altered as a result of their experiences.

Most of my father's generation is either gone or in the last stages of life. The events that shaped them, hovered in their minds, and unconsciously guided many of their reactions to later events are fading into memory. Their children, who were influenced by their parents' experiences and may have suffered trauma, are now at or close to retirement age. The passage of time brings perspective and the opportunity to view these events more dispassionately. For the grandchildren of the Shoah, it is now just a part of history to which they have a special connection.

It has been a year since his death. When I think of him lying in his coffin, I must remind myself that he taught me many useful things. When it came to the bad times, I learned what not to do as a father and a husband. Parental influence defines us, but it need not control us. He and my mother were equally responsible for giving me a sense of adventure and wonder about the world. For all of it, he had a profound impact on our lives. I would not be the same person without his and my mother's influence. I would like to change parts of my life, but I would not trade my life and experiences for anyone else's. If I say I am who I am because of them, I know a few people who would say that is not a good thing. For my mother, my wife, my brother, his children, and my children, I believe they are glad for the person I am, and their opinions are the only ones that I value. Bernard Baruch said that you should be who you are because those who mind don't matter, and those who matter don't mind. Dad would have agreed with that. Like my father, I have lived life my own way, without seeking permission from anyone. I will always thank him for that.

To the end of his life, my father did not believe that people had changed very much. The Middle East wars; the mass murders by the communists; and the slaughters in the former Yugoslavia, Cambodia, Rwanda, Ethiopia, and many other countries only confirmed his beliefs. America was the only safe place. There were just too many minorities here to concentrate all the nation's hate onto one group. That did not mean there was not injustice, only that the likelihood of mass murder was so much less.

All these survivors' families were still prone to some problems. How could they not be? Such an experience would have to leave them with a variety of ailments. Today, people who went through far less are diagnosed with post-traumatic stress disorder. These people got married, hardly knowing each other, yet they had not dealt with their demons. If they had not dealt with their own problems, how could they deal with or help each other? Counseling was generally not available, and those survivors I have known would not have taken it had it been offered. It was the Allies who betrayed Poland. It was the Germans who voted Hitler into power. It was the Soviets who enslaved half of Europe. The world, not the victims, had gone mad and needed psychiatric care.

Twenty-Four

Sometimes our fate resembles a fruit tree in winter.
Who would think that those branches would
turn green again and blossom,
but we hope it, we know it.

—JOHANN WOLFGANG VON GOETHE

My first car was a used 1974 Volkswagen Super Beetle. My father would never buy a German car. He did help me with the purchase of a used German car. He even drove it a few times when he needed a loaner. He believed that America had done a great deal for him, and buying any new foreign car put an American worker out of a job. What about parking a used German car in our driveway? He did not hate the Germans or any other group of people. The war was over; the Germans paid a heavy price, including reparations to him; and even though there would never be perfect justice, there was enough to let the past be the past. I guess if he could do that, then the rest of us can.

For a long time, I wondered if Hitler had actually won the war against the Jews. If the Shoah was always the white elephant in the room, if it was always the topic of conversation, if it was the excuse for us turning

190

our heads to some of the actions and attitudes of our parents, if the children of the survivors spend their entire lives reliving the memories of their dysfunctional families and never learn to overcome it, then it seems to me that Hitler's ghost is still lingering. It has taken time, but it has passed on for most of us. As most of the generation of survivors has passed away, there is a sense of loss that these witnesses are gone. After the grief of their loss has passed, there is a sense of relief that the "front-of-mind awareness" is no longer there. They are not forgotten. They are just not at the forefront of our consciousness.

What of the few who are still with us? My mother's memory is not what it was, but when I visit her and show her the latest pictures of her children and great-grandchildren, she is brought to tears with joy. She is especially touched, as we all are, at my grandniece Josephine. She is the first girl born in our family in two generations and named after my beloved brother.

Ever since the movie *Schindler's List* came out, Aunt Halina has been busy with public speaking engagements about her experiences. Her three children stayed close to home, and she has the joy of a houseful of grandchildren. She has always been special to me. She seemed to be the only one who spoke directly to me as a child on a level where I felt there was genuine communication. To me, there was always a feeling of gentleness in her voice, and I rarely, if ever, heard her say a bad word about another person. Given what she has gone through, there seems to be no bitterness in her or anger at anyone. For all the upheavals in my home, I always had the sense in the back of my mind that her home was somewhere I could go if I needed to. That brought me comfort and a feeling that there was a floor beneath me if all else should collapse.

Aunt Halina audits college courses at Johns Hopkins University. She raised a family. She built a successful business, but she always hungered for knowledge, and now her days are filled with the joy of learning. She married a man named David while living in the United States. She lived with my parents for a while in Omaha, Nebraska. She was tied to my father in a way that no one else in the family was, not even his wife and children. Though in love with a man from Kansas City, she was clear that she would not move away from her brother. He had been the one who rode a bike six hundred kilometers to Prague to find her and another five hundred to search for her in Krakow. She waited in Krakow for three months. She was about sixteen years old and alone until her brother and sister found her. To be separated again from her family would be impossible. It would be a long time before she met David Silber and moved to Florida, where Dave would get his master's degree and PhD in engineering.

Uncle David talked little of his war experiences. He lost all his family except for his brother, who was in Russia. Because of the Cold War, it would have been too risky for them to communicate. He was sent to Auschwitz during the war. Like Halina, he was one of the rare few who did not stay long. He was not an electrician, but like my father, who was not a watchmaker, he volunteered for a work brigade, claiming he was an electrician. When he came to Auschwitz, all his belongings were taken. He was stripped naked, and his head was shaved. They had taken everything from him, including his dignity and identity. It was at that moment he decided that if he should survive the war, he would get an education. It was the only thing that no one could take from him.

Uncle Gerry is almost eighty. He is still a professor of economics. He has been working full time longer than I have been alive, and he is still going. He wants to retire, but the lack of mental stimulation would do him in far quicker than any physical infirmities. He was a friend to me when I was a boy. He married an Israeli woman, Esther, who was as kind as she was beautiful. They brought life and joy into our home when they visited. They moved to the United States so he could continue his studies and work on his master's degree. I never saw my mother any happier than when they visited. Perhaps she saw in them the marriage that she wanted and could never have. They seemed totally devoted to each other. Gerry, the tough, macho Israeli, never seemed happier or gentler than when he was with her. I am told that despite knowing she was losing her struggle with cancer, Esther urged him to get his PhD. He took care of his wife and his two daughters and continued with his education. When she died, no one cried harder than my mother. I only saw Gerry break down for a few minutes. Between the health-care system and his schooling, he was left deeply in debt. To me, this was the time when he showed real courage.

In his poem "The Charge of the Light Brigade," Alfred, Lord Tennyson, wrote that "theirs not to reason why, theirs but to do or die." Perhaps Gerry looks back upon his military service, as do many veterans, as the happiest time in his life, because the choices are as simple as Tennyson's words. I look back upon college the same way. If I worked hard, my grades were high; if I slacked off, they dropped. It was a much simpler life then.

My mother insisted that Gerry move close to us so she could help take care of his two young daughters. He did so for their sake, even though it greatly increased his commute time to and from school. He hired help. Mom was still working. It is not as though she had the full burden, but she did a lot. It seemed like his daughters were always at our house, and they became like sisters to us. My mother's devotion to them was an inspiration to me later in life when Debbie and I were able to help an at-risk child in our own family.

Gerry was under a great deal of pressure. He had been given something precious and wonderful, and then it was snatched away from him. He tried to smile. He did his best. He taught me how to drive when I turned sixteen and, like Joe, tried to impart to me his vast wisdom about women and how to get one into bed.

When he finished his studies, he moved to Boston as a professor at Massachusetts Institute of Technology. We lost touch over the years. His daughters attended the University of Pennsylvania in Philadelphia so they could be close to my mother. After my brother's death, Gerry and I reconnected. His words of comfort, based on the lessons he learned after losing his wife over forty years earlier, were some of the kindest and most supportive I received. I had no idea that he still carried Esther in his heart, but I am glad he did.

As for my journey, Deb and I are very happy in Atlanta, where she is a professor at Emory University and I am a solo family law attorney. It was a difficult decision to move, as we had both lived much of our lives in the Philadelphia suburbs. We have two sons. One has blessed us with a grandson. We had always been close to Joe's sons. With his death, and with me as executor of his estate, we have become much closer. With Joe gone, his sons have become my sons, and their three children have become our grandchildren.

I have met many families who are proud that their child is the first in the family line to attend college, though they have lived here for several generations. As Aunt Halina pointed out to me, there is hardly a family of survivors she has known that does not have children who went to college, became professionals with advanced degrees, or enjoyed some success in business. The survivors were an example of what drive and determination mean. For the most part, they passed it along to their children.

When I was growing up, my father subscribed to a book collection called *We Were There*. It was a series of books involving a reasonably accurate depiction of an historical event. There was a youth telling a first-person account of the event. For the young lad reading the book, he could identify with the protagonist. I read *We Were There at the Alamo*, where I helped Davy Crockett reload his muskets. I was there with Ethan Allen and the Green Mountain Boys. I was there at Normandy. I was there at Gettysburg. The concept seems sort of natural, as every Passover we were there in Egypt during the Exodus. Growing up in my home, I was there during Dreyfus's court-martial. I was there when Theodore Herzl expended his life force trying to bring together all those factions into a cohesive movement. I was there in Russia with my mother every time it snowed, and she would come outside and shovel more snow faster than I could. I was there in Plaszow with my father every time he relived the story. I was in Israel with Gerry as I traveled around the country and the West Bank. I was there in 1948 every time I traveled the road between Jerusalem and Tel Aviv and saw the hulks of the makeshift armored cars that were destroyed by Palestinians and Jordanians, who shot from the high ridges around Latrun.

I was there for the 1967 liberation of Jerusalem every time I took the bus from the kibbutz down the winding road to Abu Ghosh, a Christian Arab village that had sided with the Jews in 1948. It was the village where the Ark of the Covenant rested while King David prepared Jerusalem for the Ark's entry. I was there at the Wailing Wall on Friday night when the Jews were dancing, singing, and praying while the young soldiers stood atop the wall, keeping watch over everyone. I was there on Saturday while bar-mitzvah boys stood at podiums and read the Torah amid the chaos of so many reading, chanting, and singing. The little children crawled around on the ground between the boys' legs to pick up treats being thrown by the Sephardic women, who regularly threw the candy while they made their high-pitched, tongue-wagging screams. I was dragged to tables laid out on the plaza by families of the bar-mitzvah boys who insisted I drink the whiskey and eat the food.

I was even at the Khyber Pass when the Afghans beat back the British. I was in the village of Lumbini, where the Buddha was born; and I was there at Varanasi by the Ganges, where the bodies burned; people sang; colors exploded; and men, women, and children waded into the holy waters to sing praises to their god as they had for thousands of years, with the same fervent belief in redemption as I had seen with every other religion I was exposed to. I was lucky to feel surrounded by history. I was given an inheritance beyond remuneration by my family and by my own sense of wanderlust that I had inherited from them.

The survivors were not so lucky. I came to understand that their struggle did not end with the end of the war. They struggled with their demons for the rest of their lives. There is a wise saying that dying is easy; living is the hard part. For those who were so badly scarred as they struggled to survive the Shoah, or struggled to bring a Jewish homeland into existence, nothing could be truer.

Appendix

B oryslaw. Prior to the mid-nineteenth century, Boryslaw was a village in the Ukraine, which was then controlled by Russia. It was considered part of a ring of villages and towns that were tied to the capital, Lvov. In the mid-to-late-nineteenth century, oil and a paraffin substance were discovered. It was difficult to extract. Entrepreneurial minds were needed to bring modern drilling and mining techniques to the area. The local population was not dense and was mostly involved in agriculture. Jewish businessmen came to the area, invested money and skills, and made the town prosperous. By 1880, there were 7,363 Jews in Boryslaw out of a total population of 9,318. By the turn of the century, Boryslaw was producing about 5 percent of the world's oil.

Shortly afterward, there was a major change in the technology for extracting oil. Large Austrian banks came in and purchased many of the smaller operations. The economy of scale and newer extraction techniques made it difficult for the smaller well owners to compete. Jewish workers were fired as a result of anti-Semitism, and the Jewish population declined. By 1931 the ratio of Jews to gentiles had changed dramatically. While the population grew, Jews were now only about 25 percent of the population. My family's history lies in Boryslaw. My grandfather Herschel had a small oil-well operation. After his wife died during World War I, he later remarried, left his money and property to the children and maternal grandparents of his first wife, and left for Krakow to start anew.

Chmelnitsky. Bhodan Chmelnitsky (there are other spellings), born in 1595, was a Cossack. The Cossacks were a militaristic, eastern Slavic people who settled in the Ukraine, Crimea, and Russia. Though the Ukraine was nominally under the control of the Polish-Lithuanian commonwealth during the Middle Ages, the area was lawless, and the Cossacks fought with the Ottomans, the Crimean Khanate, the Tatars, and other peoples, aside from serving with the Polish military. Some Cossacks even became leaders of the Polish army. The Poles and Lithuanians were Roman Catholic. The Cossacks were Eastern Orthodox. The Polish kings had refused to intervene in land disputes in the Ukraine. Orthodox priests were mistreated, and the Polish kings were wary of the loyalty of certain Cossack tribes. There had been Cossack revolts, and they were crushed, but Chmelnitsky's revolt would change the future of the region.

In 1648, with only a small number of men, Chmelnitsky's revolt began with an invasion of Poland. In each battle, the Cossacks serving in the Polish army defected to his side. Soon all of the Polish Cossacks were with him. He met with other Cossack tribes, united them, and was elected as their leader. He called for all Cossacks to join him, including the Ukrainian peasants whom he called slaves to the Poles and Jewish landlords. The wars that followed were indecisive. Chmelnitsky eventually made peace with the Ottomans. This allowed Russia to help the Cossacks and not risk a war on two fronts. The Ukrainians pledged their sovereignty to the czar and would eventually become part of the Russian empire. The Tatars joined the Poles and invaded the Ukraine, depopulating large regions. The Cossacks forced the Poles out. There was extreme brutality on both sides. The Poles had used Jewish middlemen to collect taxes and rents; as in other Christian countries of the time, they were the only ones who could lend money, as Christians were not allowed to charge interest. Landowners who defaulted on their loans lost their property, and the Jews now became landowners who leased the land to peasant farmers. Jesuit priests from Poland flooded the Ukraine, performing forced conversions on the Ukrainian Orthodox.

During the revolt, at Chmelnitsky's urging, the Jews were considered allies of the Poles. The numbers are disputed, but most sources put the loss of Jewish lives at one hundred thousand to two hundred thousand between 1648 and 1649—a huge number for the time that exceeded the casualties of the Crusades and the Black Death. Furthermore, the nature of the killings, involving burning, mutilation, dismemberment, and other forms of sadistic torture, was shocking even by the standards of the times. The numbers also do not include the destruction of homes, businesses, or the untold numbers sold into slavery. At the end of the uprising, and with about eight hundred thousand to one million dead, Poland, Lithuania and the Ukraine, the largest exporters of food and minerals to Western Europe, were plunged into poverty and would never recover. The Tatars, Crimeans, and Ottomans would decline with them. The balance of power in the region would flow to Russia, Austria, and Prussia.

Today in the Ukraine, Chmelnitsky is a national hero and the father of the nation. His image is on bank notes, and a large statue of him on horseback stands in the center of Lvov.

Dreyfus. Captain Alfred Dreyfus was a Jewish French military officer. He had substantial personal wealth but chose the army as a career. His family was Alsatian, an area that was lost to Germany in 1870. His family moved to France rather than live under the Germans. He was one of a breed who had come up through the newer military academies that were open to all. There was a tension in the army between the aristocrats, who had historically been the leaders by virtue of their family, and the newer officers, who rose by merit. The aristocrats brought with them their old beliefs about loyalty to the church, anti-Semitism, sentiment for the monarchy, and disdain of the republic. Dreyfus was an artillery officer. At the time, there was an arms race in the artillery between Germany and France. France had a secret program for developing a mobile 75-mm cannon that would be highly effective at close range while being small and light enough to be moved through forests, such as the Ardennes, where the Germans were likely to invade in the event of war.

French army intelligence found a letter in the trash can of a brothel, a place that Dreyfus never visited, but a poor officer of German heritage with large gambling debts by the name of Esterhazy had. The letter was on tissue paper and torn into six parts. There were no details in the letter other than that further information would be coming to the German ambassador.

The aristocratic officer in charge of the investigation targeted Dreyfus because he was in the artillery. But so were many other officers. The difference was that Dreyfus was Jewish. There was no mention of the artillery in the letter. It was an assumption on the part of the investigator that artillery was involved. The handwritings of Dreyfus and that of the famous letter did not match at all. Dreyfus had a spotless record and received many recommendations from his superiors. As a Jew, however, it was supposed he had an innate cleverness, a lack of loyalty, and even the genius to purposefully make sure the handwritings were so dissimilar that he must have been the author. While being a Jew was not brought up at trial, the handwriting analysis was. His personality was used against him, which could be used against any person. There was even hearsay testimony presented from a secret source whom Dreyfus was not allowed to confront.

France became divided between the Dreyfusards (who supported Dreyfus) and the anti-Dreyfusards. The vitriol, false accusations, and anti-Semitic propaganda written by right-wing papers and church-affiliated sources were intense. Still, both Dreyfus and his supporters believed in the French justice system, and only a fair trial could ensue. Because of their belief in French justice, they had no doubts that he would be found innocent. After all, there was no real evidence that he had done anything wrong. Instead, without one piece of hard evidence and no motive, he was convicted in 1894. He was sentenced to live on Devil's Island, chained to a wooden bed. He grew weak and despaired of ever seeing his home again.

In 1896, under pressure from Dreyfusard politicians and newspapers, the army's persecution and lack of evidence came to light, casting doubt on the military leadership. A new investigation was ordered. When it confirmed not only that Dreyfus was innocent, but that Esterhazy was the real spy, the upper classes felt the need to convict Dreyfus again, not because he was guilty, but for the greater good of the nation. They believed it was in France's interest that the people not lose faith in their military leaders, even if an individual had to be sacrificed. In their minds, it was simply one more reason why the Jew was disloyal. He only thought of himself. He was a coward who refused to sacrifice himself for the good of the country. After all, isn't that what being a soldier is all about?

Dreyfus was paroled in 1896 after being convicted again. There were anti-Jewish riots in over twenty French cities, including Paris, all in the name of liberty, equality, and fraternity. Not until 1906 was Dreyfus reinstated in the army and promoted to major. He fought in World War I and ended his career shortly afterward with the rank of lieutenant colonel. The effects of the Dreyfus affair cannot be underestimated in the clarification of the ideals of the Zionists. For many, France was the heart of civilization, the center of culture, art, beauty, free thought, philosophy, and egalitarianism. Here, the Zionists could see that no matter the level of achievement or assimilation, the dark side of anti-Semitism could erupt at any time. If Jews could not be safe here, they could not be safe anywhere in Europe.

Herzl. Theodor Herzl was from a wealthy, assimilated, German-speaking Jewish family from Pest in Hungary, then under the control of the Austrian Empire. His ties to Judaism were tenuous. He had no bar mitzvah and no religion, and he treated Judaism with cynical disregard. He was completely secular, and his writings show he was probably an atheist. He studied law in Vienna. He became a journalist and playwright. While writing for a newspaper in Paris during the Dreyfus affair, he witnessed the French mobs screaming, "Kill the Jews!" Though he considered Dreyfus guilty, as almost everyone did after his first conviction, he came to change his mind when the truth started to come out.

He was also influenced by the election of Karl Lueger in 1895 as mayor of Vienna, a city that Herzl came to regard as his hometown, a city as refined, beautiful, and cultured as Paris. Lueger had founded the Christian Social Party and championed anti-Semitism as part of his populist politics. His party became the model for the Nazis. Both the Prime Minister of Austria and Emperor Franz Joseph opposed the sanctioning of his electoral victory, but after two years, Pope Leo XIII intervened on Lueger's behalf, and his election was finally sanctioned.

Herzl wrote *Der Judenstadt* (*The Jewish Land*) in 1896. For existing Zionists, he became the new leader, the one who could articulate a dream. For the Orthodox and the liberal-assimilated Jews, Herzl was a source of controversy. Herzl had come to the belief that anti-Semitism could not be eradicated, and the only solution was for Jews to remove themselves from Europe for a new homeland, possibly in Argentina, British East Africa, or Palestine. He believed Palestine was the best choice, as it was more inspirational and would attract more immigrants, but he was more than willing to consider other alternatives to achieve his dream. Herzl now spent all his time, inheritance, and health on promoting his Zionist visions. He met several times with the German kaiser, including a meeting during a trip to Jerusalem since the kaiser had influence with the Turks.

Herzl eventually met with the sultan of the Turkish Empire. He presented a plan where the Jews would pay off the Turkish national debt, thereby making them independent of foreign countries, and bring in the brightest minds to manage Turkish finances that could only make their economy stronger and more independent. His offer was rejected, but the Turks had no particular problem with Jewish émigrés who paid their taxes and followed the laws. He also met with representatives of the Vatican but was essentially told that it was not the policy of the church to advocate for those who rejected the divinity of Christ.

He established the First Zionist Congress in Basel, Switzerland, in 1898. He became the first president of a Jewish organization with extremely diverse political views and representing a multitude of nationalities. In Basel, he predicted that in fifty years, the Jews would have their own homeland. He was on target. He also believed that anti-Semitism would grow. He was alive for the pogroms the czar's government had instituted as a way of relieving the pressure from reformists. He never predicted anything as unimaginable as the Shoah, but he was driven by his lack of faith that European society would ever allow true equality, no matter what contribution the Jews made. He died in 1904 at age thirty-four and was buried in his family plot in a humble ceremony. He requested his body only be moved to the new Jewish homeland after its establishment. His body rests in a simple tomb in Jerusalem with only his name on the side of his stone sarcophagus.

Krakow. Krakow is Poland's second-largest city and began as a stone-age settlement. Krakow became the capital of Poland. In the early fourteenth century, King Casimir III (the Great) granted privileges to the Jews, forbidding the kidnapping of Jewish children for the purpose of forced baptism as well as desecration of Jewish cemeteries and houses of worship. While Spain, England, and France had expelled the Jews, he allowed large numbers of Jews into Poland and protected them as "people of the king." As a result, about 70 percent of the world's Ashkenazic Jews can trace their ancestry to Poland. Jewish immigration to the Polish-Lithuanian Commonwealth brought an explosion of prosperity. The Jews had previously settled in a suburb created by Casimir called Kazimierz. He allowed them to build walls around their community for protection. In time, as Krakow grew, Kazimierz was incorporated into the city of Krakow, and many Jews left Kazimierz to live in other parts of the city. The majority stayed in Kazimierz, as it was the center of the Jewish community. The more observant Jews stayed due to the prohibition of traveling on the Sabbath, so they would be close to their synagogues. After Poland declared its independence at the end of World War

I, Krakow became the cultural center for Polish Jewry and the home of a large Zionist youth movement.

With the Nazi occupation, Krakow became the capital of the General Government, a separate administrative region from the rest of Poland, under Hans Frank. The Poles, and many Germans, often referred to Krakow as "little Paris." Hans Frank was so charmed by the city that he created a Jewish ghetto outside the city limits so that the city would remain pristine, unlike Warsaw and other Polish cities.

Frank was a typically brutal Nazi administrator, persecuting and murdering both Jews and Poles while looting all the wealth of the city and its inhabitants. His goal was to eventually rid the city of all Poles and Jews. Frank protected the city, and despite some looting by the Russians, by the end of the war, Krakow was relatively unscathed. The Jews died in the horrid conditions of the ghetto, were sent to extermination camps, or sent to the Plaszow concentration camp. Today, Krakow is a United Nations World Heritage site.

Lebensraum. This is a German word that literally means "life room" or, as understood in the west, "living space." It was nothing more than a form of social Darwinism, which the colonial powers had used as justification for taking territory. The concept was not a product of Nazism. It was a major impetus for World War I. The Germans would annex western France, where the iron ore was mined. They would move eastward and annex part of Poland and perhaps move even further. They had almost achieved their goal, first in taking western France and, later, at the Treaty of Brest-Litovsk in 1918 (where the Bolsheviks gave up their claim to Poland), the Ukraine and the Baltic states.

The idea behind lebensraum was that Germany had a growing superior population of industrious, healthy, intelligent people. The other races, particularly in Eastern Europe, were populated by an inferior people with high birthrates that would eventually encroach on German lands, mixing and debasing the Germans just as the barbarians had with the Romans. These lands were to be depopulated by forced expulsion so that Germany would be free to grow and become self-sufficient in agricultural and mineral resources.

The Nazis took this a step further. According to Hitler, Germany was overpopulated because of the boundaries set by the Treaty of Versailles. The Germans were the master race or *ubermenschen*. The Slavic people in the east, along with the Roma and the Jews, were inferior races or *untermenschen*. The Nazis used the United States as an example. Europe was overpopulated. Nordic (English) people moved to America, where land was plentiful. Their sense of national purpose led them to expand westward. The land spread from one ocean to the other, and those inferior races, the Native Americans, were either exterminated or so reduced in number as to no longer be a threat. The Nazis planned to move into Eastern Europe and exterminate the Slavic peoples, leaving only a small number as slaves to work the fields and labor in the mines. Germany's survival would be guaranteed.

Molotov-Ribbentrop Pact. Molotov was the foreign minister for the Soviet Union, and Ribbentrop was his German counterpart. Though the West was aware of this nonaggression pact, signed on August 23, 1939, they did not know of the secret component that, in return for Stalin's acquiescence to the German invasion, would allow Russia to invade areas of Poland and the Baltic states that had been part of the Russian Empire prior to the treaty of Brest-Litovsk in 1918. The West was stunned by the news. The two nations were historical enemies. Fascism and communism were the ideologies of enemies. Each was sworn to wipe out the other. As long as the two countries were enemies, the West had felt safe. As long as they believed Hitler would move eastward into Poland and Russia, there would be no chance of war. The French and English were still weary from World War I. They had no desire for war, even if they had to betray their Polish ally.

For the Germans, the reasons for the pact were straightforward. Germany wanted to invade Poland and was not yet ready for a war with the Soviets. The West had never understood Hitler's brinkmanship and always believed that Germany was more powerful than it actually was. When the Germans invaded the Rhineland, they had almost no ammunition to fight with and were ordered to withdraw if the French attacked, but the French did nothing. In the Sudetenland, the Germans marched in with only a few rounds per soldier. Again, they were to withdraw if they encountered major resistance. Hitler simply relied on his assumption that the democracies were weak and had no stomach for a fight.

Stalin's reasons were more complicated. His paranoia led him to kill most of his experienced army officers. He wanted to promote the peasants, who would owe him their absolute loyalty, but they had no experience as officers. Stalin's equipment, artillery, tanks, and air force were inferior to the Germans'. During the 1930s, growth in agriculture and industry was behind expectations. Stalin's forced collectivization policy of industry and agriculture was, at first, a disaster. The Ukraine, famous as the "bread basket of Europe," contained an agricultural community of middle-class farmers, as did much of the Soviet Union. They were called Kulaks; and, had they been left alone, they would have formed a large, loyal middle class. Instead, those who resisted were killed, imprisoned, or exiled. In the Ukraine, the farmers were required to surrender most of their crops. They resisted and hid their crops from collection. The army came in and confiscated their crops, their farm equipment, and machinery. The whole Soviet Ukraine was left to starve by the millions.

Stalin needed time. Agricultural and industrial production were slowly rising. He needed time to move his factories east to the Urals in case of a German invasion. He needed three years to build more modern tanks and planes. He needed the time to give his new officers experience in command. He needed the time to reorganize the army from traditional static defense to the more modern dynamic defense. Traditionally, there was no artillery corps, and even with the development of tanks, there was no tank corps. Artillery and tanks were assigned to army units for their use. These weapons could not be reassigned as needed during battle, as they belonged to those army units to which they were assigned. Germany, on the other hand, had already created a dynamic system by creating a separate artillery corps and tank corps under the authority of the general staff of the army. This meant that tanks and artillery could be moved within the interior lines as needed.

By the time of the German invasion, Stalin still needed two more years. He was desperate for time, and the Molotov-Ribbentrop pact would give him that time, or so he thought. German intelligence was aware of the Soviet army's backwardness. They struck in June 1941, before the Soviets were ready.

Shoah. Throughout this book I have used the word "Shoah" in place of the word "Holocaust." The word "Shoah," in Modern Hebrew, literally means "catastrophe." There is no other way to describe what happened. There is nothing especially wrong with the use of the word "Holocaust." It has come to mean the same thing. It is the more popular word among Jews and gentiles. However, "holocaust" is a Greek word, not Hebrew. It literally means "wholly consumed by fire," in the sense of a sacrifice. The concept of redemption through death is simply not part of modern Jewish thought. The idea that there is some redeeming quality to the murder of so many, especially one million children, minimizes the suffering and the horrific loss of life to the European Jewish community. Any community that lost two-thirds of its members through murder has suffered nothing less than a catastrophe. Christians may mourn the death of their people as they wish. If they choose to place crosses at concentration camps, or believe there was a redeeming power in the sacrifice of Christian victims, they are certainly entitled to their beliefs. We cannot Christianize or Judaize the Holocaust. Each community that suffered must interpret it according to its traditions and beliefs. As a matter of respect to my family members who lost so much, I choose to use the word "Shoah" for Nazi or Nazi-inspired persecution of the Jews just prior to, during, and immediately after World War II, rather than the word "Holocaust."